C000271619

THE SEVEN AGES OF MAN

The Seven Ages of Man

How to Live a Meaningful Life

James Innes-Smith

CONSTABLE

CONSTABLE

First published in Great Britain in 2020 by Constable

1 3 5 7 9 10 8 6 4 2

Copyright © James Innes-Smith, 2020

The moral right of the author has been asserted.

All rights reserved.
No part of this publication may be reproduced, stored in a retrieval system,
or transmitted, in any form, or by any means, without the prior permission in
writing of the publisher, nor be otherwise circulated in any form of binding or
cover other than that in which it is published and without a similar condition
including this condition being imposed on the subsequent purchaser.

A CIP catalogue record for this book
is available from the British Library.

ISBN: 978-1-47212-995-6 (hardback)

Typeset in Bembo Std by SX Composing DTP, Rayleigh, Essex
Printed and bound in Great Britain by Clays Ltd, Elcograf, S.p.A.

Papers used by Constable are from well-managed forests
and other responsible sources.

Constable
An imprint of
Little, Brown Book Group
Carmelite House
50 Victoria Embankment
London EC4Y 0DZ

An Hachette UK Company
www.hachette.co.uk

www.littlebrown.co.uk

For my father

CONTENTS

Introduction
The Crisis of Meaning

What is the purpose of your life here on earth? Is it simply to grab as much as you can before you die, or do you yearn for something more? Man's greatest challenge is to find meaning in a seemingly random universe, to get beyond the sort of rampant materialism and greedy self-interest that has singularly failed to quell our deeper yearnings. All over the world men are waking up to the fact that for life to have meaning they must accept certain fundamental truths: that actions have consequences, rights come with responsibilities and fulfilment lies in the service of others.

Over the past fifty or so years, the West has been busily dismantling many of the institutions and moral frameworks designed to foster these deeply humanising ideals. In our frenzied pursuit of self-actualisation, we have managed to replace humility and civic duty with ego-driven autonomy and narcissistic desire. 'I' rather than 'we' took hold of our better natures, leaving us bereft of purpose and isolated from each other.

Most of us have an instinct for what matters in life, but without a clear roadmap, it is all too easy to drown in life's shallow end. But we mustn't give up on our quest. Those who pursue meaning are generally more content, have fewer negative emotions and a lower risk of mental illness. Our higher purpose therefore must be to dive deeper, to reconnect with our better natures and embrace a modest life defined by clear moral boundaries, committed relationships and putting other people's needs before our own.

We need each other in profound and moving ways, ways that appear to be at odds with the twenty-first-century ideal of radical autonomy. Paradoxically a new form of tribalism based on group identity, immutable characteristics and competing power structures has taken hold, removing us even further from the idea of a civil society based on trust, forgiveness and mutual respect. A parallel, equally febrile gender war has been fracturing the delicate relationship between men and women built up over millennia.

From the trauma of two world wars and the erosion of unifying institutions such as marriage and organised religion to profound cultural changes and the undermining of traditional masculinity, the last century and a half has been a particularly turbulent time to be a man. But turbulent times demand honest reflection, clear thinking and sound advice free from the bitterness and recrimination that has tainted so much recent discourse.

As men, we need to renew our commitment to fundamental freedoms of speech, thought and conscience, along with a redis-covery of forgotten values such as decency, courage, self-sacrifice, honour and grace. And while it is important to embrace change where change is due, we mustn't lose sight of our collective past and the lessons and insights handed down to us from previous generations.

Because every stage of life presents its own unique set of challenges, I have taken William Shakespeare's 'Seven Ages of Man' speech from *As You Like It* as a guide. Making the long and perilous journey from 'mewling and puking' infant to 'lean and slipper'd' decrepitude takes courage, determination and a clear head. I hope this book will help you navigate your way through the strange complexities, moral dichotomies and maddening contradictions of modern-day life.

A Brief History of Modern Man

Throughout the Victorian period, men tended to adhere to a strict set of masculine ideals; these included pride in work, religious devotion, good manners and chivalrousness within marriage. For all their fey sentimentality, the Victorians were actually great admirers of traditional 'manliness', which they saw as the glue holding society together.

As head of the household, a man's primary duty lay in protecting his family. Gender roles remained clearly defined, with women expected to stay home and care for the children while men went out to work. But by the second half of the nineteenth century, the focus had begun to shift away from the Protestant work ethic and strict religious adherence towards what became known as 'muscular Christianity', characterised by a belief in patriotic duty, discipline, self-sacrifice, and the moral and physical benefits of athleticism. In order to educate the mind, one also had to focus on the body. The prioritising of competitive games, as played out on the sports fields of major public schools, was seen by those in authority as the ultimate arena in which male competency could thrive – if you were good at games, it naturally followed you would be good at life.

Sporty boys were treated as potential leaders of men and defenders of empire, while those lacking the requisite prowess often found themselves ridiculed, bullied and marginalised. When it came to robust masculinity, Victorians recognised in Charles Darwin's evolutionary thinking a vision of the world that seemed to fit their own social ideals. Victorian England's belief in survival of the fittest meant that by the turn of the twentieth century there existed an entire generation of men described by E. M. Forster as having 'well-developed bodies, fairly developed minds, and undeveloped hearts', qualities that would prove useful in the traumatic years that followed.[1]

The mass slaughter of young men over the course of two world wars had such a profound effect on the male psyche that the trauma still resonates across men's collective consciousness even now. Practically every British man alive today will have lost someone: a grandfather, great-grandfather, cousin or great-uncle in one or other of the two world wars. As with all bereavements, society is still trying to come to terms with the loss, unable to comprehend the full magnitude of what happened. More than 100 years have passed since the outbreak of the Great War, and yet the idea of self-sacrifice remains deeply ingrained within men's subconscious, as evidenced by the dangerous, backbreaking work still predominantly carried out by males.

The relatives of those men who did make it back from the front line faced a whole new set of challenges. Post-industrialism had largely decimated the manual labour derived from heavy-manufacturing industries, reducing the status of low-income males and weakening the 'national social contract' that had bound communities together since the Industrial Revolution.

Mass-employment industries such as coal mining and ship-building, for so long the bedrock of working-class life, either went into severe decline or moved elsewhere.

Outside the world of work, men were struggling to adapt to sweeping cultural changes too. The 1960s were not only about challenging social norms and traditional hierarchies, they also marked the dismantling of long-held, clearly defined gender roles and a loosening of morals which many men found uncomfortable and disorientating. A profound shift brought about by women's liberation, the contraceptive pill and changing attitudes to marriage and employment meant men could no longer rely on the sort of historic precedence that had kept them grounded for so long.

With the disappearance of well-paid manual labour, unqual-ified men found themselves at a loss economically. The service industries that took the place of heavy manufacturing in the 1980s and '90s appeared to favour female talents, revealing a remarkable turnaround in women's fortunes and a distinct downturn in men's, although an ongoing debate about the gender pay gap suggests there are still anomalies within the system. The global economy had evolved in such a way as to erode the his-torical preference for male children worldwide. In 2010, females had become the majority of the workforce for the first time in US history.[2] For every two men receiving a college degree that year, three women would do the same. Even strictly patriarchal countries such as South Korea were seeing a dramatic transfer of power as industrialisation took hold. The same gender shift was occurring in other rapidly industrialising countries, includ-ing India and China, as well as in advanced economies such as the UK and USA.

Statistics showed that women earned more doctoral degrees and were now a majority of those entering medical and law schools. Young men were dropping out of university and falling behind in the workplace. Single women were two and a half times more likely to buy their own homes, while single men more often lived with their parents. The Western post-industrial economy appeared to be far more conducive to female talents. Masculinity had reached a moment of existential crisis. The beginning of the twenty-first century saw a spike in mental-health issues, with suicide becoming the biggest killer of men under forty-five, far higher than that of women. While the media tended to focus on mental-health issues in young men, older, middle-aged males were also suffering. Labelled the 'buffer generation' in a 2012 Samaritans report, midlife males often found themselves sandwiched between two sets of competing ideals.[3] On one side were the older baby-boomer men, now in their sixties and seventies, inheritors of stoic, stiff-upper-lipped masculinity handed down from post-Victorian fathers and grandfathers. As a demographic these men tended to struggle with emotional articulacy, while at the same time feeling the need to conform to strict masculine templates.

However, despite some obvious limitations, baby boomers benefitted from a clear set of inherited principles. They knew who they were and what was expected of them. With the help of male-centric spaces such as gentlemen's clubs, working-men's clubs and provincial Rotarian and sports associations, older men had the advantage of being able to let off steam and validate their sense of masculinity within an historic and established framework. By contrast, generation X (born between the early 1960s and late '70s) and millennials (born between the early 1980s and late '90s) seemed disaffected and directionless. Millennials in particular were being encouraged to see themselves not as biologically defined, 'heteronormative' males but as part of an ever-expanding range of 'masculinities' notably free from established virtues once seen as an essential part of every functioning male.

Increasing numbers of young men found themselves anchorless, uprooted from the conventions and certainties of their forefathers. A lack of moral clarity along with a blurring of boundaries had left their mark on what looked increasingly like an abandoned generation of youths.

Over the past decade or so, masculinity itself has come under attack, adding further to the confusion. Men were said to be the progeny of unenlightened empire-building bigots and the inheritors of undeserved 'male privilege'. They belonged to an 'oppressive patriarchy' that lorded it over women and minorities through a socially constructed, tyrannical hierarchy. Those seeking an end to male dominance cited the likes of Harvey Weinstein and Donald Trump as examples of a virulent form of 'toxic masculinity' sweeping the world. Campaigning organisations such as Me Too and Time's Up[4] sought to expose an ongoing culture of assault and sexual harassment within certain industries and across society more broadly.[5] As well as bringing the guilty to justice, campaigners sought to change men's behaviour by challenging society's understanding of maleness. Men needed to atone for historical injustices, reject 'traditional' and 'toxic' forms of masculinity, and accept that gender was little more than a socially constructed lifestyle choice. We had arrived at a crucial turning point in our history, with men being asked to reflect on their past and prepare for a radical new intersectional dawn where the old rules no longer applied. Society's tectonic plates were shifting once again.

Act One
Childhood

Mewling and puking in the nurse's arms

For centuries, the nuclear family has been the bedrock of civil society. It has defined our values and shaped who we are as a nation. But rising divorce rates and a breakdown of the traditional family unit is fundamentally changing the way we raise our children. This in turn has had a profound effect on broader society and the way men and women interact with each other.

The question of whether boys need their biological fathers has become a particularly divisive issue. Those from less conventional households, such as single parents and same-sex couples, argue that as long as boys are loved and feel secure then it shouldn't matter whether there is a father present, biological or otherwise. While it is undoubtedly true that love is the most important ingredient for any relationship and that unloving or violent fathers are bad for children, the evidence from leading authorities such as Dr Warren Farrell, author of *The Boy Crisis*, suggests that boys are more emotionally balanced and have better life chances when there is a biological father at home.[1] Notwithstanding the evidence, same-sex couples and single mothers are understandably concerned that they might suffer discrimination if such lifestyles become stigmatised. While no one should deny there are viable alternatives to the nuclear template, there needs to be a proper discussion about what is best for children free from ideological or cultural concerns. We live in morally ambivalent times, so people in power are reluctant to promote one set of values over another, even if the evidence appears to favour a particular position. It's a tricky dilemma but one that needs to be addressed. If we value the stability and well-being of children, then perhaps it is our duty to follow the evidence regardless of any moral ramifications or possible hurt feelings. A healthy, functioning nuclear family offers balance, firm foundations and a particular set of principles designed to foster long-term stability. Without these strong familial ties, children can sometimes lack the security and consistency they need for a contented upbringing. As we have witnessed over recent decades, society pays a heavy price when these established bonds start to crumble.

In purely monetary terms, the 2016 update of the Relationships Foundation's 'Cost of Family Failure Index'[2] showed that the price of family breakdown to the taxpayer stood at £48 billion, costing each citizen around £1,820 a year. That's a total of forty new schools per annum. But family breakdown is far more than just a heavy financial burden.

In *The Boy Crisis*, Dr Farrell sees a rise in fatherlessness as a major contributing factor to the health and well-being of young men. Farrell blames the downgrading of marriage, easy divorce and feckless fathers for the growth in male delinquency, violence, depression, underachievement and even terrorism, with vulnerable, fatherless boys often deliberately targeted by terrorist organisations such as ISIS.

On average, single parenthood exposes children to much higher economic instability. The number of single-parent households in poverty, for instance, is much higher than for parents who stay together. Farrell's findings also show that 'dad-deprived' boys tend to suffer emotionally more than those brought up within traditional nuclear families. For example, for unmarried couples who break up, 40 per cent of the fathers fail to have contact with their children after two years, leading to trauma for those left behind. And fatherless boys are less likely to display empathy and assertiveness and are more likely to be disruptive and even homicidal. According to a UNICEF report on the well-being of children in economically advantaged countries, including the UK, 85 per cent of youths in prison have an absent father.[3] The shortage of male teachers across the entire education system means fatherless boys lack any kind of intimate male role model. The Centre for Social Justice (CSJ) statistics show that 1.1 million young people have little or no contact with their fathers.[4] Children in some of our poorest communities are growing up without any male role models. The CSJ describe this lack of male influence as 'an ignored form of deprivation', which can have 'profoundly damaging consequences on social and mental development'. The report goes on to reveal that there are now 'men deserts' in many parts of our towns and cities. Across England one in four state-primary schools have no full-time qualified male teacher and 80 per cent of state-educated boys are in primary schools with three or fewer full-time qualified male teachers. An area in the Manor Castle ward of Sheffield, which tops the lone-parent league table, showed that among households with dependent children, 75 per cent are headed by a lone parent (most commonly a woman). According to the CSJ, father absence is linked to higher rates of teenage crime, pregnancy and disadvantage. Director Christian Guy has warned of the 'tsunami' of family breakdown battering the UK: 'The tragedy of family break-up is devastating children, parents and communities.' Yet faced with what he describes as a national emergency, the response from politicians from both the left and right has been 'feeble'.

Another study by the clinical psychologist Jenny Taylor looked at why a proportion of boys with all the risk factors associated with criminal behaviour resisted a life of crime.[5] Drawing on data from socially deprived areas of south London, she compared a group of well-behaved 'good boys' without any criminal convictions, with a group of 'bad boys' at a secure unit for unmanageable adolescents, many of them persistent offenders. The most striking difference between the two groups showed that 55 per cent of the 'good boys' lived with their biological fathers, compared with only 4 per cent of the 'bad boys'. Almost 80 per cent of the 'good boys' spoke of being close to their biological fathers. Among these were 24 per cent of the group who said they had a biological father living away from home but who remained a strong influence in their lives. The study showed that a father who makes it clear that he disapproves of crime and bad behaviour while demonstrating an active interest in his son's well-being acted as a vital social control, countering negative influences. The fear of losing their father's love and approval was enough to deter boys from crime. As such, Taylor suggests we should move away from pathologising single mothers and instead concentrate on the damage caused by absent fathers.

Academics aren't the only ones who recognise the harm being inflicted on dad-deprived boys. A growing number of concerned women have started campaigning on behalf of boys caught in the trauma of family breakdown. Belinda Brown from the organisation Men for Tomorrow works with men and boys caught in what she sees as an unfair justice system.[6] Like many working in the field, she questions why authorities are failing to make a connection between gang-related knife crime and fatherlessness, despite the fact that most of the offenders come from broken homes.

After regularly visiting Feltham Young Offenders Institute in London, Labour MP for Tottenham David Lammy, whose own father walked out on him, said he found that most, if not all, offenders did not have access to their fathers. Former gang member Sheldon Thomas, the founder and chief executive of Gangsline Foundation Trust, a non-profit organisation established in 2007 to provide assistance to young people involved in gang culture, said he agreed with Mr Lammy 100 per cent, citing 'bad parenting, absent fathers and bad male role models' as the biggest problems when tackling knife crime. 'Successive governments refused to look at the important role that fathers play in any community,' Thomas said, adding that 'the moral factors and the values of this country have completely changed'.[7] In 2011, Addaction, a charity specialising in drug and alcohol problems among young people, warned of an epidemic of 'father-hunger'. The report revealed that we were witnessing a social time bomb of subconscious anger that needed to be treated as a public-health issue.[8] Back in 1965, the American politician Daniel Patrick Moynihan warned that 'a community that allows a large number of men to grow up in broken families, dominated by women, never acquiring any stable relationship to male authority, never acquiring any set of rational expectations about the future – that community asks for and gets chaos'.[9]

Sonia Shaljean, meanwhile, saw the link between father-lessness and offending during her career in the Metropolitan Police, where she managed a Community Safety Unit and helped refer victims and perpetrators to the right services. As founder of the award-winning community-interest company Lads Need Dads, she worries about the number of vulnerable men growing up without a responsible, stable father figure. The organisation's team of male mentors encourage emotional intelligence in vulnerable fatherless boys aged eleven to fifteen, while providing opportunities for youngsters to take part in outdoor activities, learn practical skills and volunteer in the community. The aim of Lads Need Dads is to provide support, guidance, encouragement and a much-needed male voice to enable boys to open up emotionally during traumatic break-ups. Through careful mentoring, boys' self-esteem begins to grow, they become more emotionally stable and motivated, and they will often perform better at school. Relationships at home improve too.[10]

So, what sort of influence should you as a biological father bring to bear on your son, and how do you make sure your little boy has the best chance in life?

Birth and early childhood

There's no reason why a father's input shouldn't begin on day one. Being at the birth of your child can be a momentous occasion, although some men may feel out of their depth. Witnessing those first few seconds of birth can be wonderfully bonding for both parents, but if you are squeamish in any way, you may want to wait outside with a stiff drink. Giving birth can be a traumatic and undignified affair, so your wife should have the final say on whether you get to stick around.

During those first couple of years, toddlers are like little sponges – they pick up on everything, so be mindful of how you behave around them. Watch your language and try not to row with your spouse when the little one is within earshot. Bad language has become so normalised in our society that most of us don't even realise we are doing it. In certain contexts, such as poetry and literature, expletives are a necessary form of creative expression. During everyday speech, however, obscenity coarsens interactions and can be especially demoralising for children to hear. The 'f' bomb and 'c' word have both lost their power to shock and are now little more than a dispiriting, lazy form of speech.

Intimacy is vitally important from day one, so don't forget to look your little boy in the eye and tell him how much you love him. There's no need to feel soppy or embarrassed; toddlers crave affection from both parents, so give your child plenty of hugs, tickles and kisses, even if you were starved of emotional warmth yourself. When denied outward expressions of love, children may struggle to form intimate relationships in later life, but you should also avoid showering them with gifts. Kids need consistency. It's tempting to express affection through the giving of toys but resist the urge no matter how much he pesters. Presents are a poor substitute for genuine expressions of love. Remember, children spoil easily, so try to turn every gift into a rare treat and don't be over-generous or he'll lose perspective and become over-entitled. Instead of buying him garish, mass-produced tat, try to feed his creativity by challenging him to make something of his own. Provide him with materials and tools and see what he comes up with. Don't forget to praise his efforts, however mad or surreal. Eccentricity shows he has flair and imagination.

On the question of whether 'gendered' toys perpetuate stereotypes, try not to force your son to wear pink and play with dolls if he prefers to wear blue and play with trolls. Likewise, if he shows a propensity for sparkly outfits and fluffy unicorns, try not to be judgemental. All children go through phases.

Building resilience

Soon your child will be walking and talking and looking to you for inspiration, so be patient and feed his enquiring mind with positive nuggets of wisdom and watch in wonder as his unique personality starts to take shape.

The importance of play should never be underestimated. Nor should play-fighting, which starts during the toddler years and continues through to late primary school. Also known as rough-and-tumble play, horseplay and roughhousing, this form of pretend scrapping is a great way for children to learn about empathy and boundaries. Some parents discourage play-fighting because they worry about cuts and bruises, but getting knocked about is all part of the learning process. It's how children become socialised.

During rough-and-tumble sessions, boys will often test each other's strength by taking it in turns to play victim and perpetrator. This helps them establish where the boundaries of acceptable behaviour lie. By their early teens, play-fighting will have dropped away, but for those first few years, don't be afraid to bond with your boy over a good-natured scrap, but remember to reprimand him if he crosses a line.

The issue of whether or not we should allow our children to play outside unattended has divided opinion in recent years. A heightened, often exaggerated fear of 'stranger danger' means increasing numbers of kids never get the opportunity to enjoy the freedom of the great outdoors, even though the odds of them being abducted are extremely slim – around 300,000–1 according to official figures.[11] The charity Action Against Abduction estimates that roughly fifty children under the age of sixteen are abducted by strangers every year in the UK, while NSPCC figures show that more than 90 per cent of kidnapping and child sexual abuse is actually perpetrated by someone known to the child.[12] Parents do their boys a terrible disservice by keeping them hermetically sealed from the perceived dangers of the outside world.

From about the age of seven, children love to explore, either on their own or with friends, so try not to become paranoid. It's perfectly normal to feel protective of children when they are out in public, but they are much safer than you think. Cocooning them from the vagaries of real life will only weaken their resolve in adulthood. Apart from the fun of being away from prying parental eyes, playing outside helps kids forge their independence. Even if you live in a city, there's no reason why your children shouldn't go off exploring on their own as long as they are made aware of the dangers. Encourage them to play in local parks and to avoid busy roads. Giving boys a long leash encourages them to stand on their own two feet. Of course, they will get into all sorts of scrapes along the way, but that's how they learn to use their initiative. Try to look upon grazed knees and bruised elbows not as wounds but as lessons learnt. Experiencing and overcoming pain is one of the primary ways children build the sort of resilience they will need to cope with hardship later in life. Without the occasional bruised ego how else are young people supposed to learn about humility and restraint?

Schooling

It's never too early to teach your child about the difference between right and wrong. A rise in moral relativism, along with a fear some of us have of not wanting to seem judgemental, has left children increasingly confused about what's expected of them. Many schools, particularly in the state sector, have become wary of imposing discipline, fearing it might limit self-expression. In 2017, the UK government launched a five-week consultation period on its guidance for expelling and exclusions in schools. The most common reason cited for both permanent and fixed-period exclusions was 'persistent disruptive bad behaviour'.[13] This is not necessarily teachers' fault. Over many years, they have seen their authority eroded by the implementation of strict human-rights regulations. Once children are made aware of these protective rights, they will often use them as justification for errant behaviour. Fearing reprisals from over-protective parents, teachers often choose to ignore low-level disruption until it escalates into outright anarchy. It's important therefore for both teachers and parents to think of discipline less as a punishment and more of a guiding influence.

For some within the teaching profession, discipline has become synonymous with stifling, Victorian authoritarianism in which sadistic headmasters physically abuse hapless waifs for the slightest misdemeanour. But this *Tom Brown's School Days* caricature of authority is outdated and misleading.[14] It may be an unfashionable position to espouse, but discipline is as vital for healthy child development as nutritious food, physical and cognitive exercises, unconditional love, and a home in which to live. According to Dr Farrell, children yearn for rules – it's how they learn to negotiate the complexities of the world around them. Denied discipline, children lack the basic tools necessary to forge successful relationships. They will often struggle to face up to life's challenges, such as respecting others, self-discipline, deferred gratification and cooperating with peers. It's easy to spot those who haven't been regularly disciplined, as they are usually the most inarticulate, disruptive and resentful boys in the classroom. Undisciplined children are often unpleasant to be around and will most likely struggle to make friends. Clinical psychologist and psychoanalyst Dr Stephen Blumenthal believes that boys in particular need boundaries in order to feel safe: 'Without discipline they inhabit a chaotic, frightening world devoid of structure. Boys who transgress without consequence often suffer the most.' Applying clearly defined rules helps to rein in testosterone's aggressive and sexual impulses, helping boys focus their energies elsewhere.

It's crucial that children learn how to manage their own behaviour and regulate any negative impulses. Since the birth of the progressive education movement in the 1960s, schools have been particularly remiss when it comes to enforcing discipline, and this laxity has had a marked effect on children's ability to learn and grow. If you are worried, find out if the teachers in your school are fulfilling their duty to maintain order in the classroom. If discipline is not being maintained, think about the implications for your child's future and if possible, find another school.

Some educationalists espouse an anti-competitive ideology in which 'all must have prizes', blurring the link between hard work and achievement. Many primary schools, for instance, have sought to emphasise 'taking part' rather than 'winning' across every aspect of school life, from academics to sport.[15]

While this may work for brighter children, a healthy, level-headed approach to competition can help encourage less driven pupils to make more of an effort. Businessman and politician Sir Digby Jones argues that a culture of anti-competitiveness is creating a generation ill prepared for a world that requires risk taking in order to function effectively. He has said that competition teaches critical thinking, decision making and problem solving. Of course, being competitive doesn't mean trampling all over your opponent. Lyn Kendall of British Mensa has talked about the importance of competition within a supportive framework, where children can learn to accept failure, but without losing their confidence and self-esteem.[16] Team sports is a good example of where competition thrives on fair play and cooperation rather than individuals winning at any cost. Without the drive to succeed, young men can lose their sense of purpose.

When it comes to your child's understanding of gender identity, you need to be aware that highly politicised social-justice organisations such as Stonewall and the Good Lad Initiative have been infiltrating schools across the UK in a bid to influence young minds. Good Lad, for instance, hold regular workshops that encourage boys to reject traditional masculinity and embrace a muscular, anti-patriarchal form of feminism and a socially constructed gender ideology, leaving many impressionable, pre-pubescent boys confused about what it means to be a man. The initiative's focus on eradicating toxic masculinity presumably adds to a sense of masculine dysfunction.[17] In 2020, Good Lad planned to launch an 'Anti-Patriarchy Club for Boys', recruiting young men mainly from schools and training them in 'anti-oppression work'. Perhaps you welcome such a move, but if you have doubts, arrange to speak with a representative. Question what they mean by 'patriarchy' and ask them what relevance this loaded term has with regards to your child's education – are they suggesting, for example, that all male power is tyrannical and therefore needs to end? Make sure any outside influences are being properly monitored and assessed. Ask to sit in on a workshop if you feel you'd like to know more.

In a similar vein, schools advocating 'diversity and inclusion' policies that go beyond the need to call out individual cases of bigotry may be pushing an identity-politics ideology that judges human beings according to a sliding scale of victimhood. This fashionable doctrine, also widespread across many universities, often makes sweeping assumptions about 'male privilege' and the systematic oppression of minorities while ignoring the complex circumstances of individual lives. By focusing entirely on broad immutable characteristics, schools are sometimes failing to take into consideration other, more nuanced forms of prejudice and inequality that have yet to make it onto the statute books. Class, wealth, upbringing, health and geography can all have a significant impact on a child's life chances, regardless of gender or ethnicity. There are numerous other factors at play that can also leave children at a disadvantage – attractiveness, intelligence and personality, for example. While there is no doubt that gender and racial discrimination still exist, most twenty-first-century disadvantage stems from poverty, deprivation and family breakdown; cure these ills and the rest will usually follow.

Likewise, if your son is being asked to attend workshops in 'unconscious bias', 'heteronormativity' and 'white privilege', make sure you are aware of the context in which these disciplines are being taught and the reasoning behind them. By 'decolonising' the curriculum, many schools and universities are failing to offer a balanced history of Western civilisation. Schools that advocate such policies are not only denying your child's heritage but also damaging their ability to think critically.

If history lessons focus too heavily on the evils of empire while ignoring our cultural and historical achievements, then take note. Question the school if you feel your child isn't receiving an objective, all-round education.

Here are a few more buzzwords and stock phrases to look out for when assessing school policy:

- Teachers may talk about 'conversations' being 'framed' by a 'narrative' or 'paradigm'. Question the use of jargon more generally in schools (and in all other areas of life) – these baffling words and phrases are often used to deflect, obfuscate and confuse laypeople. Note that ideologues are particularly partial to jargon when laying out their intentions.

- If teachers are asking males to 'make space' for women and minorities, this could be seen as a form of discrimination that has no place in schools. Boys should not automatically be discriminated against because of the gender they happen to have been born into. Surely a child can be made aware of historical inequality without being held responsible.

Teachers may dismiss traditional Western 'narratives' as 'the stories we tell', insinuating that historical facts are a matter of opinion or part of an oppressive Western patriarchal construction. The word 'community' might sound benign, but it is commonly used to divide individuals into homogenised groups or tribes, as in the 'black', 'LGBTQ' or 'disabled' 'community', the assumption being that minority groups all think and feel a certain way. This patronisingly reductive and paternalistic way of viewing difference is a form of control that encourages victimhood and spreads division. The words 'inclusivity', 'equity' (equality of outcome), 'tolerance' and 'diversity' have taken on almost religious significance in schools and universities, so be on your guard and don't be afraid to ask awkward questions such as:

What does 'equality of outcome' actually mean in practice, and how do you encourage children to make an effort if all must win prizes?

Where does 'tolerance' begin and end, and who gets to decide?

Is there such a thing as too much diversity, and why should diversity of immutable characteristics trump diversity of ideas and opinions?

Does 'inclusivity' only apply to minority groups, and if so, what are they being included into?

Are children being asked to judge each other on their immutable characteristics rather than the content of their characters?

(Note: You may find yourself asking the same tough questions in Act Four, where similar 'diversity and inclusion' initiatives are being rolled out across many of our major institutions and corporations.)

Remember, teachers should be inspiring pupils to think beyond narrow tribal allegiances and the limitations of their own circumstances, imbuing them with big ideas, broad intellectual enquiry and the wonders of history, art and civilisation. You need to show some courage, especially when it comes to your child's education. Don't simply go along with fashionable orthodoxies – if you feel strongly about the way your school is being run (the same applies to universities in Act Two), speak out. Make sure you know exactly what your child is being taught and why.

The number of boys dropping out of school or leaving without basic numeracy and literacy skills is a national scandal but one that few in power dare speak about. Trevor Phillips, former chairman of the Equality and Human Rights Commission, blames a 'lethal cocktail of inverted snobbery, racial victimhood and liberal guilt' for the reluctance to help educate white boys in particular, whom he describes as today's 'educational left-behinds': 'I doubt that I'll ever work out why the British appear untroubled that so many of their children emerge from over a decade of expensive, compulsory education with scarcely more in the way of literacy and numeracy than the average Neanderthal.'[18]

Why we should celebrate the beauty of language

In the UK, speaking clear, educated English has become synonymous with class division, snobbishness and elitism, which could explain the lack of educational rigour when it comes to teaching the language. You may have noticed the extent of adolescent inarticulacy when listening to school leavers struggling to construct a coherent sentence without constantly falling back on phrases such as 'like' and 'you know what I mean'. Titans of the spoken word such as Stephen Fry argue that since language is constantly evolving, we shouldn't obsess over petty niceties such as fluency and grammar.[19] Children must be free to develop their own patois unencumbered by outdated rules and conventions. But neglecting to teach basic language skills leaves children woefully ill-equipped to function in the real world. They can only riff on language once they know the ground rules. Instead of lowering standards to meet ideological whims or cultural and class sensitivities we should be lifting boys out of the prison of low expectation, equipping them with the tools they need to live a fulfilling and communicative life. Every pupil has the right to leave school with a strong command of the English language regardless of class or privilege. Without vital literacy skills, your child will struggle to find purpose and meaning. Not only will they be denied access to all the great works of literature, they will often struggle to communicate clearly, making it difficult to find gainful employment. A 2018 National Literacy Trust report on the link between literacy and life expectancy shows that children growing up in areas with high levels of illiteracy are more likely to be unemployed, have low incomes and poor health, leading to significantly shorter lifespans.[20] With social mobility severely compromised, your illiterate child will become increasingly resentful about the lack of opportunities afforded them and with some justification. It's vital therefore that you encourage them to read from an early age and don't be afraid to call out sloppy speech. Articulacy is a vital, civilising skill that will be of great benefit to him throughout his life. As well as feeding your child's imagination, reading them a bedtime story will also imbue them with a love of language.

If your child is struggling to read, write or speak coherently, meet with the head teacher to find out why. Perhaps they are being disruptive, or maybe the school is failing in its duty to educate. This may not always be the teacher's fault. So much of the curriculum has become about bureaucratic box ticking and a manic need to hit targets, all of which detract from core learning. Successive governments have shamelessly used education to advance their own interests, culminating in a relentless stream of new policies and initiatives that have resulted in intrusive levels of meddling and less learning time. With class sizes growing, it has become increasingly hard for teachers to engage with pupils. So, stay involved and make sure your child isn't missing out.

The importance of self-discipline

As boys enter adolescence and those turbulent teenage years, they will be much better equipped to overcome difficulties and resist temptation if they have the tools to encourage self-discipline. It is therefore the duty of parents as well as teachers to set a good example by instilling decency, good manners and sound moral values. Setting clear boundaries unlocks children's better natures and teaches them the value of restraint. Playing by the rules encourages civility and empathy, allowing your children to fulfil their potential.

Firm foundations

For centuries, the Church of England lay at the heart of community life in Britain. Although Brits have always shied away from describing themselves as 'religious', churchgoing remained an important part of civic life up until relatively recently. According to the Office for National Statistics there were 4 million fewer

Christians in 2011 than 2001. Despite our loose affiliation with the established church, most of us appreciated the importance of the message; loving your neighbour as yourself, compassion for the weak and faith in something beyond the limits of the self just seemed to make sense.

Even without the awkward religious bit, Christianity offered a solid foundation and a clear set of values that anyone with a sense of civic duty could espouse. The constancy and transcendent beauty of church and cathedral architecture remained a comforting reminder to anyone willing to look up that there was something beyond the drudgery and disappointment of our earthly existence. But in recent decades, as society has fractured and our faith in faith has declined, we have struggled to find any kind of meaningful replacement. Our dogged belief in secular acquisition and personal gratification has consistently failed to fill the hole left by our religious heritage. As a result, we have become unmoored from life's deeper truths. Values instilled in our ancestors – thriftiness, good manners, stoicism and neighbourliness – have been gradually eroded.

Polls consistently show that the richer and more secular we become, the less contented we are.[21] Indeed, those who acquire the most are often the least fulfilled, the emptiness of acquisition intensifying the more we accumulate. Perhaps our blind faith in consumerism's worn-out dream is a form of self-protection; breaking ranks and forging our own path to meaning feels too risky. We may have an instinct for what matters, but how can we be right and the rest of the world be wrong? And so we continue shuffling down the well-worn path of least resistance, along with everyone else, in the vague hope that we might finally crack the code to secular fulfilment, while all around us forests of Babelian glass and steel remind us of our folly.

Hope may spring eternal, but we should remain wary of herd instincts that too often end in a stampede to the bottom. When considering how to raise your child, spare a thought for their spiritual well-being. Christian heritage is part of the fabric of British society, its influence can be seen all around us, in our culture, politics and morality.

If you are wondering what values to instil in your boy, reflect on your own life. Try to pinpoint when and where you have felt most fulfilled. Chances are, these rare but profound moments will have occurred while you were putting other people's needs before your own, or when you were helping those less fortunate. Often, we find fulfilment and meaning in the company of friends and family, or when we are visiting a sick neighbour in hospital. Being in nature gives us profound insights and a sense of perspective, while transcendent art keeps us spiritually nourished. All the great religions and philosophies espouse these meaningful, life-affirming truths, so once you become aware of the things that have given your life meaning, try to imbue your child with the same high ideals.

Deep down we all recognise meaning; we feel it in our hearts, and it touches us in profound ways. During times of reflection, remember the importance of your spiritual and cul-tural heritage, and ask yourself whether GDPs, fiscal projections and positive-growth forecasts can ever replace that yearning for deep connection, spiritual succour and a sense of place.

You don't have to convert your son to a particular religion necessarily, but there is much to be learnt from the simple yet profound truths embedded within the tenets of our established church. Remind him that these spiritual values have bound our society together through times of tragedy and conflict, whether we were practising the religion or not. Spiritual awareness and a belief in certain moral imperatives will give your child a firm foundation from which to find purpose and meaning.

Standing on his own two feet

Wherever possible, persuade your son to walk or cycle to school. Apart from keeping him physically fit, it will help him gain confidence, and he will learn to use his initiative. And remember there can be no growth without risk taking. Children will be in a much better position to adapt to changing circumstances once they learn to overcome their fear of taking on a challenge.

Diet

Introduce your child to delicious, nutritional food early on – this will ensure he follows a healthy diet into adulthood. Avoid indulging his sweet tooth – according to official NHS guidelines, consuming too much sugar can lead to obesity and tooth decay.[22] Children aged seven to ten should have no more than twenty-four grams (six sugar cubes) a day, while children aged between four and six should have no more than nineteen grams (five sugar cubes). Food manufacturers tend to overload certain products with sugar in order to attract younger consumers. A single can of cola, for instance, can contain as much as nine cubes of sugar, more than the daily limit for adults. When out shopping, always check nutrition labels and go for the reduced or lower-sugar options. A Diabetes UK report shows that the number of obese adults in England has risen from 6.9 million in 1997 to around 13 million in 2017.[23] This worrying trend is the most significant driver for new cases of type 2 diabetes, accounting for up to 85 per cent of risk. The disease is responsible for serious health conditions that can lead to blindness and even amputations. Gluttony often begins in childhood, so try to instil healthy eating habits by providing plenty of fresh fruit and vegetables and maintaining strict portion control.

Imagination

Encourage creativity from day one. For instance, children are naturally musical, but instead of wasting time and money on generic piano lessons, allow him to make his own discoveries. If he loves jazz, for example, he might discover an affinity for drumming or the trumpet. Once he has found his metier, that will be the time to start nurturing his talent. Arrange for him to have lessons with an inspiring teacher and set aside a space for him to practise (sound-proofing recommended). Introduce your boy to a broad range of musical styles, from major classical composers to the latest singer-songwriters. Be discerning when it comes to popular music and avoid genres that revel in aggressive nihilism or generic, meaningless pap churned out by cynical record labels. For example, 1960s jazz, '70s soul/funk and classic '70s rock offer substance, musicianship and emotional resonance.

Have some Beethoven playing in the background during mealtimes, and a bit of Bach at bedtime will soothe away jangled nerves. Imbue your child with harmonious sounds, and have fun together dancing and singing along to your favourite tracks. His passion for music will most likely happen through osmosis, so you don't have to force anything. Apply the same rules for all other creative endeavours. Plaster his bedroom walls with posters of old-master paintings and modernist classics alongside action-hero favourites. Set aside an easel, a few canvases and a box of gouache paints and allow his creative juices to flow. Instil in him a love of books by filling his bedroom with modern classics, from Roald Dahl to Philip Pullman. Encourage his creative talents and be enthusiastic whenever he shows promise. Boys thrive on words of affirmation, so be generous with your praise.

A note on why culture matters

Great art shouldn't be the sole preserve of a rich, educated minority, and you should question those who denigrate high culture as 'elitist', 'irrelevant' or 'inaccessible'. Like all meaningful undertakings, the appreciation of art isn't always easy, but that should never be a barrier to access. Many of our creative institutions are losing faith in complexity and the idea that they are there to enlighten rather than simply reflect. As a result, high art is being dumbed down in the patronising belief that ordinary people are not up to the challenge. Avoid limiting your child's imagination and introduce him to difficult concepts early on. We need to raise children's expectations not dampen them.

Get to know your son while he's at his most curious

Take him fishing. Go to the park and kick a football around. Hike together, share ideas and find out what he thinks about all the important stuff. He may only be six, but he will already be forming strong opinions and be fascinated by the world around him. Be discerning; it's never too early to introduce your son to philosophy and big ideas. Buy him a telescope so he can marvel at the vastness of the universe and a microscope for minute explorations. Never talk down to him or patronise him with baby voices. Speak to your boy as you would an adult while maintaining your authority. He needs to be able to look up to you but without feeling intimidated.

Pets

Buy him a dog and watch his eyes light up. Explain how dogs live in the moment and that he should follow their example. We could all benefit from becoming more like dogs.

Friendships

Throw regular parties for your child. A willingness and ability to make friends in Act One will stand him in good stead for forming deeper, lifelong connections in Acts Three, Four and Five. Encourage him to be gregarious and to be himself around other people.

Knowing that he's not the most important person in the world will come as a great relief and will help build his self-confidence. Shyness can stem from caring too much about what other people think, so remind him that everyone else is just as insecure as he is and not to worry.

Make sure he doesn't take himself too seriously

Self-effacement and a sense of humour are vital tools he will need throughout his life. Pablo Neruda called laughter the 'language of the soul'. Those who are unwilling or unable to laugh at themselves are often censorious and intolerant of other people's failures and foibles. Keep reminding your son of his own ridiculousness and of life's innate absurdities. Explain that we are all crazy in our own ways. Encourage him to value seriousness without losing his sense of fun. Gently introduce him to the concept of his own mortality and explain that death is nothing to be feared.

As a parent, it's easy to forget that every action, every decision you take, however small, has an influence on your child's development and future well-being. Children look to us for guidance in every area of life, from what to eat to how to think to when to go to bed at night, so it's important to keep reminding ourselves of the profound responsibility that comes with parenting. Examine the way you were brought up and note down all the things that have had a negative impact on your life and try not to fall into the same trap. Your parents' best intentions may have been misguided, so it's important to develop the parenting skills that work best for you and your child. As you look back, try not to become embittered by your parents' failures and fallibilities and assume that they were trying their best. Keep reminding yourself of the mistakes they made and then do everything in your power to break the chain of familial dysfunction. Above all cherish these innocent times together. They'll be over before you know it, and you'll miss them when they're gone.

Childhood – in summary

- Teach your child how to think, not what to think
- Remember, children need boundaries and discipline
- Remind them of the importance of not taking themselves too seriously
- Explain the difference between right and wrong
- Remind them of the importance of friendships, and encourage them to be gregarious
- Celebrate the beauty of the English language, and pick them up on grammar and spelling mistakes – articulacy is a civilising influence
- Make sure schools are fulfilling their duty to offer an all-round education free from political doctrines
- Teach your son to ride a bike as soon as you can so he can build his confidence and go off exploring
- Encourage outdoor play as much as possible
- Don't force your offspring to be creative but instead lay down threads that lead them into a relationship with meaningful experiences that last – feed their imagination
- Remind them of their spiritual heritage
- Encourage resilience through rough-and-tumble play
- Read to them at night
- Cherish every moment

Act Two
Adolescence

Creeping like snail unwillingly to school

All adolescent males feel they are misunderstood, and for good reason. Transitioning from carefree boy to responsible man can be a strange and isolating experience. It's tempting to treat adolescents as grown-ups, even though they might not feel ready to join the complexities of the adult world quite yet. The closer we come to adulthood the more alien it can seem. Everything feels unfamiliar and hostile to our needs. We find ourselves caught between the comfort and security of childhood and the seductive but unfamiliar freedoms of adulthood. The body meanwhile is taking on a mind of its own, morphing into something unrecognisably 'you'. The many physical, sexual, cognitive, social and emotional changes that occur during this time can cause anxiety for everyone concerned. Guiding your child through the choppy straits of adolescence to the calmer waters of adulthood takes hard work and perseverance.

The World Health Organization (WHO) defines an adolescent as any person aged between ten and nineteen.[1] Giving young people a gestation period during which they transition into adulthood acts as a useful buffer zone, a place where children can make mistakes as they find their adult feet. And while this period of uncertainty serves a useful purpose, we need to remember that adolescence is supposed to be a means to an end rather than a destination in itself. Some have interpreted the Peter Pan story, for example, as a warning to adults about the perils of never growing up.[2] Many of us, however, have bought into the more romantic aspects of the story without heeding some of the cautionary elements. The fallout from this state of perpetual adolescence is all around us, in our infantilised media and across the political sphere, where politicians dumb down their message in order to appeal to the youth vote. The trouble is, when we fail to make the leap into adulthood, we abandon the idea of responsibility. Encouraging children to remain in a state of suspended childhood damages their life-chances. In his book *The Vanishing American Adult*, author and academic Ben Sasse has shown that in times of peace and prosperity it is not enough for parents to simply sit by and allow reality to wake their children into adulthood. While we should be grateful for the fact that our kids are growing up in the richest, safest time in human history, we need to make them aware of their own mortality, because as Sasse points out, 'scar tissue is the foundation of future character'. Teens need to appreciate the joys of birth and growth but also the tragedy of pain and decline. In the current climate, Sasse believes they are becoming increasingly ignorant of the latter.[3]

Throughout history young men have benefitted from rites-of-passage ceremonies where adults gave clear instructions on what was required of them in adulthood. The Ancient Greeks, for instance, practised Hermeticism, during which responsible elders mentored adolescent boys, introducing them to manly pursuits such as hunting, philosophy and martial arts. In the UK, fathers used to engage in formal chats with their offspring, where they would reiterate the importance of responsibility, duty and restraint, particularly around sexual matters. With the exception of Jewish bar mitzvahs, rites-of-passage ceremonies have largely disappeared in the UK, where the transition is marked by a first legal pint (or five) at best. Because the duties and responsibilities of adulthood are so rarely discussed, some young men see no reason to grow up, remaining in a permanent state of adolescent denial.

Sasse notes that for the first time in human history children are living segregated lives, where many fifteen year olds only ever mix with other fifteen year olds and parents are increasingly absent from the transitioning process. This lack of integration with elders such as grandparents means children are entering adulthood with no concept of their own mortality. How are thirteen year olds ever to become wise if they spend all their time with other thirteen year olds? Enforced segregation means children are growing up in a protective bubble in which they lack perspective and struggle to deal with concepts such as pain and suffering. Often there will be a surplus of material wealth but without the benefit of experiencing hardship. A diminishing work ethic driven by deindustrialisation along with a precarious jobs market can lead to dysfunctional adulthood.

Amid all the acne and anguish, adolescent boys desperately seek our guidance, even though they pretend not to. And it is this need for clarity and leadership that is sadly missing from so many young men's lives. Fathers are failing to live up to their responsibilities as children struggle to make sense of the moral vacuum we have created for them.

Many of the rules, protections and disciplines designed to guide adolescent boys through life's tricky second act have either been condemned as cruel and outdated or abandoned altogether. Young men are crying out for spiritual and moral guidance, but we have torn up the roadmap. Instead we parrot empty, individualistic platitudes. We tell them to 'be free', to 'follow your heart' and 'be true to yourself', yet these are meaningless concepts to young people who have yet to develop a sense of self. Moral uncertainty and a breakdown of trust have replaced ancient traditions and fatherly advice.

By fetishising youthful folly, infantilised adults have undermined their own authority. The bond of trust between adolescents and adults has been upended, with teachers and parents now desperate for young people's approval rather than the other way around.

Politicians focus on young voters who have yet to form coherent opinions on important subjects. For instance, the UK Labour Party has pledged to lower the voting age to sixteen, effectively allowing children to have their say on complex social and economic issues.[4] Meanwhile, the entertainment industry is now so in thrall to the youthful dollar that it ignores great swathes of the adult population. Streaming services such as Netflix and Amazon follow the marketing adage that if you get young people hooked early on, they are yours for life. Big-budget series tend to stick to well-worn themes such as young women's autonomy or young men's sci-fi fantasies. Cinema is dominated by superhero franchises, while the major studios churn out big-budget cartoons aimed squarely at the tween market.

Meanwhile, record companies have largely given up investing time and money nurturing the sort of grown-up bands that value musicianship over style and attitude. Instead, the charts are full of generic, computer-generated urban-dance tracks that play well to the youthful club scene. When culture no longer reflects what it means to be an adult, young people become trapped in a kind of Adult Deficit Disorder.

Responsible male role models have been in such short supply of late that youths increasingly look to footballers, rappers and YouTube bloggers for guidance, many of whom lack the rectitude young people crave. As our immature and increasingly desperate mainstream culture coarsens and fragments, young men naturally gravitate to the sort of content that plays to their baser instincts. It is our job as adults to steer them away from these negative influences.

Gang culture, knife crime, truancy, easy access to pornography, violent video games, a lack of discipline and respect for authority, addiction and mental health issues, a coarsened attitude to sex and relationships, inarticulacy, and a debased and infantilised media — all these social and cultural anomalies can be traced back to our failure to behave like responsible adults.

Our retreat from personal responsibility has resulted in a catastrophic failure of duty to protect young men in particular. And we do them no favours by pathologising and debunking the whole idea of masculinity, as was the case in August 2018 when the American Psychological Association issued one of the most controversial reports in its 125-year history. Drawing on forty years of research, the dense 30,000-word document, the first of its kind, concluded that 'traditional' masculinity was 'harmful' for men, women and minorities. Released in the wake of the Me Too movement and designed for mental-health professionals working with boys and men, the report maintained that males who were socialised to conform to 'traditional masculinity ideology' were often negatively affected in terms of mental and physical health. Toxic masculinity, the report argued, had infected society and needed to be stamped out. Widely regarded as a global leading authority on men's mental health, the APA analysis represented the most thorough investigation into masculinity ever undertaken. The guidelines acted as a mission statement for the organisation's 117,000 members, which included the majority of practising psychologists. In January 2019, six months after that initial, rather muted launch, the APA tweeted a condensed version of the report, outlining the inherent dangers of 'heteronormative masculinity', described as 'a particular constellation of standards that have held sway over large segments of the population, including anti-femininity, achievement, eschewal of the appearance of weakness, and adventure, risk and violence'.[5]

The study leaves out some of the more positive aspects of traditional masculinity, such as resilience, stoicism and bravery, qualities that have benefitted both men and women throughout the centuries. At the same time the APA fails to address serious issues concerning poverty, loneliness, existential doubt and self-esteem. If you tell young people they are privileged simply by dint of their gender, then is it any wonder that their self-confidence is shattered when they look in the mirror and fail to recognise the accusations levelled at them.

Psychologists and male-behaviour specialists remain split over the usefulness of the APA report. Writing in the British Psychological Society magazine *The Psychologist*, Dr Stephen Blumenthal, Consultant Clinical Psychologist and Psychoanalyst, alerts colleagues to what he sees as the dangers of the APA guidelines, which he describes as 'a crude application of critical gender theory to the clinical needs of males'. Quoting the APA description of 'traditional masculine ideology' as a constellation of negative standards, Blumenthal maintains that 'this odd collection of symptoms implies that achievement and a spirit of adventure is pathological and synonymous with violence'. While we tend to think of women as being on the wrong side of gender inequality, Blumenthal argues that when it comes to health and educational performance, the reality is often the reverse: infant mortality, for instance, is higher in boys, while males are at greater risk of premature death.[6] Across the world, boys are much less likely to reach standards of proficiency in reading, maths and science. Criminality and suicide are predominantly a male preserve.

American physician, scientist and author Randolph Nesse goes even further by suggesting that being male is the single largest demographic factor for early death.[7] While Blumenthal acknowledges the necessity for considering the clinical needs of males as listed by the guidelines, he finds it 'startling' that the APA would go on to attribute what he describes as 'excessively unfavourable statistics' to an ideology that 'traditional masculinity – marked by stoicism, competitiveness, dominance and aggression – is, on the whole, harmful'. In Blumenthal's opinion, the clinical role of psychologists is to treat patients rather than indoctrinate them. He argues that the APA completely miss the clinical wood for the political trees, rejecting what he sees as the infiltration of critical gender theory into psychological practice 'where everything is attributed to social construction and nothing is rooted in nature'. Blumenthal worries that male dysfunctions are being attributed to a particular social construction of masculinity that is apparently rooted in 'patriarchy' and 'white supremacy', and where political re-education is seen as an appropriate cure.

He notes that the 30,000-word report doesn't contain a single reference to 'testosterone', even though the male sex hormone is shown to have a profound effect on men's self-esteem, sex drive and mental health. Blumenthal's clinical and research experience in treating men who have suffered and who cause suffering to others concludes that their anger and misuse of power shouldn't be blamed on a distorted ideology but is instead often the consequence of abuse or neglect.

If the APA have their way, Blumenthal worries that we could end up living in a 'sterile, grey, lifeless world in which men are pacified, submissive and emasculated'. He would prefer to see a world in which we celebrate equality with difference. It is hard enough to engage men and boys in addressing the psychological obstacles that inhibit their lives. The APA guidelines, he concludes, succeed in 'alienating half the species, many of whom are in desperate need of psychological help'.

To counter unhealthy and demoralising narratives you need to keep reminding your son that there is no shame in being a man and that he should celebrate the achievements of his forefathers.

Adolescent males face a particular set of challenges as they struggle to come to terms with hormonal changes and a world that expects them to stand on their own two feet. Young men are particularly impressionable at this age, so it's important to steer them away from harmful, debasing influences.

Overcoming smartphone, gaming and social-media addiction

Resist buying your son a tablet or smartphone for as long as you can. This may well be one of the biggest dilemmas you face as a parent, but it's important to allow your boy to discover the rich diversity of the physical world before succumbing to a pixelated facsimile. So much of the digital world has been designed to keep young men glued to their screens. Seeing as we are still grappling with the rapidity with which these devices have taken over our lives we should err on the side of caution.

Up until the launch of the iPhone in 2007, the digital landscape had remained pretty barren. Facebook and Twitter were still in their infancy and seen by many as a passing fad. Mobiles were little more than landline extensions with a few add-ons, such as texting and a poorly conceived camera that nobody used. If you wanted to check emails, you had to go home and fire up your bulky PC. In-phone gaming was limited to chasing pixelated snakes across the tiny black-and-white screen of your underpowered, overpriced Nokia 6110. The iPhone was a literal game-changer, with the number of apps rocketing from a mere 500 at the launch of the app store in 2008 to nearly 1.85 million by 2020, 265,793 of which were mobile gaming apps.[8]

The digital world soon began to dominate every facet of life, from banking to shopping to watching movies. We had everything at our fingertips, and anything seemed possible. Young men were early adopters of the new technology, abandoning clunky old gaming consoles for the ease and convenience of a pocket-sized gaming device. By 2009 innocent snake-chasing had morphed into deeply immersive, long-form platform games with complex often violent storylines all available free of charge, although 'free' often came at a price. In order for gamers to progress through ever-trickier levels, they had to purchase in-game credits. These 'freemium' games could end up costing parents a fortune on credit-card bills. It was a brilliant strategy as far as the gaming corporations were concerned. First, you give away your product, then once the consumer is hooked you start charging them for their addiction. A lack of proper regulation means the business model continues to encourage prolific spending and addictive behaviour in adolescent males, distracting them from more meaningful endeavours. Gaming may seem like a bit of harmless fun, but the days of gathering around a Space Invaders machine down at the local arcade are long gone. In-phone gaming is now a multimillion-pound business, with young men as the chief consumers. The Association of Interactive Entertainment values the UK gaming market at a record £5.7 billion.[9] According to a report by the research firm NPD Group, smartphones and tablets are now the most popular devices used for gaming among children aged between two and seventeen.[10]

While gaming eats away at young men's precious time, social media narrows their horizons by encouraging isolation, self-absorption and a retreat into tribalism. Nobody is yet sure what the long-term effects of smartphone addiction might be, but the constant stream of garish imagery, scattergun news feeds, frenetic, violent gaming and anxiety-inducing social media appears to be addling young men's minds and eroding vital social skills. The Office for National Statistics has found a 'clear association' between longer time spent on social media and mental-health problems. While 12 per cent of children who spend no time on social-networking websites on a normal school day have symptoms of mental ill health, that figure rises to 27 per cent for those who are on the sites for three or more hours a day.[11] Excessive internet use may prevent young people from developing strong relationships offline. If your son is addicted to his phone or tablet, take action now and don't allow him to become a prisoner of his own device.

It takes courage to row against the tide of popular culture. Young men are desperate to fit in, so convincing your son to abandon his device won't be easy. You could start by telling him to be his own man and to stop following the herd. Ask him if he really wants to be held hostage by a gadget designed to dominate his life. If he already has a smartphone, limit his screen time using all the parental controls you have at your disposal and remind him of all the other, more edifying things he could be doing with his time. If he's in his mid to late teens, for instance, buy him a tent and some sturdy walking boots and encourage him to go hiking with his friends.

Gaining a sense of perspective through deferred gratification

We live in an age of instant gratification. The immediacy of the digital world means we now expect everything to be on tap, from deliveries and ready meals to sex and romance. A sense of entitlement pervades our culture. Waiting is for losers.

Adolescent boys in particular struggle with the whole concept of delayed gratification, but instead of teaching them about the importance of short-term sacrifice for long-term gain, we have been indulging their impetuous natures. You need to remind your son of why a gratification delayed is a gratification gained. In order for him to live a meaningful life he has to understand that true fulfilment takes time and effort. Unlike video games and social media, real life isn't about adrenalin rushes and instant fun.

If your son is skipping school or thinking about dropping out of university because he is bored, gently point out that if he works hard now the chances are he will have a much more fulfilling future. Teach your boy about the benefits of restraint in every aspect of life, from sex and relationships to work and leisure (this is where your efforts to instil discipline and responsibility in Act One really pay off).

Once your son has learnt to temper his desires, he will start to appreciate the simple things in life. As he learns to overcome challenges, he will gain humility and a sense of perspective. Small victories will seem like substantial gains and waiting will no longer feel like a waste of time.

A note on toxic masculinity

In recent years, 'traditional' masculinity has come under attack from activists who view gender as a social construct. The behaviour of men like Harvey Weinstein and Donald Trump is seen as indicative of a toxic inheritance found in all men. While it's important to root out such behaviour, the sad truth is there will always be power-hungry tyrants willing to abuse their position, but that does not mean we should all be judged by their standards. If your son is anxious about gender, focus his attention on some of the more positive aspects of being a man. 'Traditional' masculinity, for instance, may have certain macho connotations, but it also includes attributes such as stoicism, strength, courage, independence, leadership, heroism and assertiveness, essential virtues for any man willing to risk death and serious injury in the service of others. While young women are encouraged to be brave, courageous and strong, these same qualities are often seen as 'problematic' in young men.

University life

If your son manages to gain a place at university, encourage him to work hard and to think for himself. Remind him that the whole point of higher education is to broaden his intellectual horizons by introducing him to a wide range of views and opinions, some of which he may find controversial or even offensive. Teach him to value free speech and to question lecturers who may have an agenda to push. Make sure he listens respectfully and in good faith to what others have to say and encourage him to articulate his viewpoints calmly and clearly without resorting to abuse or ad hominem. Remind him that debates about important issues are rarely black and white and that you never win an argument by cancelling or shutting down your opponent.

Choosing the right university course

Parents sometimes fall into the trap of using their children's education as a way to make up for their own frustrated ambitions. But just because you failed as a doctor doesn't mean you have the right to pressurise your child into reading medicine. Allow your kids to develop their own interests and support them in whatever fields of study they choose. You might think their decision to read history of art, for instance, is misguided, leaving them with few employment opportunities. You may be right, but that's for them to decide. Do you really want to deny them the possibility of studying a subject they feel passionate about simply because you are worried about a future no one can predict? Offer your child advice when needed, but learn to trust their instincts too. Pay particular attention to courses that have 'theory' or 'studies' in the title as in 'critical race theory' and 'queer studies' – make sure you interrogate the purpose of these disciplines fully before enrolling.

Resisting gang culture and knife crime

A 2019 report by the Children's Commissioner estimated that 27,000 children in England aged between ten and fifteen considered themselves to be in a gang.[12] Adolescent boys yearn for order and a sense of belonging. Joining a gang gives vulnerable young men in particular the sort of discipline they crave. A 2008 report by a teachers' union blames family breakdown and a lack of father figures for pupils joining gangs.[13] Increasing numbers of children are living insecure, chaotic lives devoid of meaning and purpose. Gang life offers them the security that may have been missing from their family life, which is ironic considering the nihilistic tendencies shown by gang leaders.

Despite the violence and criminality, young men who join gangs gain the same set of principles found in most functioning households. They quickly learn to respect their elders (gang leaders), they do what they're told (on pain of punishment), they are tasked with duties (selling drugs) and they are rewarded with a sense of belonging.

The spread of gang culture is another serious indictment of our parenting skills and of teachers' failure to inspire. If we are to dissuade vulnerable young men from joining gangs, we need to offer them a more meaningful alternative. Bunging them a few quid and the odd 'youth club' while at the same time fetishising and celebrating the sort of nihilistic, antisocial behaviour that encourages gang culture simply isn't good enough. We need to be raising young men's expectations by introducing them to a world of possibilities beyond their immediate surroundings. Focusing attention on our shared historical and cultural inheritance gives them something tangible to be proud of. It also cuts across class divides. Adolescent boys are particularly vulnerable to outside influences, so if you fail to offer them an alternative path to meaning, they will gravitate to the lowest common denominator. By encouraging them to put other people's needs before their own, troubled young minds will eventually come to realise the hollowness of gang culture.

Expand adolescent minds with a grand tour

Your child has been born into one of the most remarkable civilisations in history. Encourage them to explore, honour and celebrate their inheritance by sending them on a grand tour of European cities. This can be done relatively inexpensively with an InterRail pass that gives anyone under the age of twenty-seven one month of unlimited train travel to more than 40,000 destinations across thirty-three European countries. Make sure their itinerary includes Florence, Rome, Athens, Venice, Paris and Vienna, cities where European culture reached its zenith. Remind them how lucky they are and to be grateful for such an extraordinary legacy.

A note on the dangers of ideological groupthink

Two thousand years ago, Socrates wrote that when citizens assess arguments on merit rather than through the prism of ideology, democracy flourishes.

Avoiding coarse popular culture

When societies fracture, we tend to lose sight of who we are and what we believe in. As old certainties and long-held traditions start to fade from view, we cast around for a safe harbour, yearning for a return to sanity and order. During uncertain times, we may abandon hope and wallow in despair. It's vital therefore to hold on to all those civilising influences that make life seem bearable. Culture has the power to lift us out of our malaise and show us a world beyond imperfect reality and the fragile self. By embracing philosophy, literature and the creative arts we nourish our better natures, allowing hope to return once again. Our broken society is crying out for a return to meaning and an appreciation of what really matters, but instead of consoling us with deep, life-affirming truths, jaded cultural arbiters have chosen to mirror our existential despair and exaggerate the sense of hopelessness.

Many art-gallery owners, for instance, have become inured to baffling installations by artists who appear to wallow in mocking audience sensibilities while laughing in the face of craftsmanship and transcendent beauty. Meanwhile, architects are paid to construct brutally utilitarian edifices on an unwelcomingly inhuman scale that appear to reflect our own sense of desolation. In the world of music and fashion, young, impressionable women are conned into believing that the only way to feel truly empowered is to flaunt their sexuality along sleazy, industry-led standards that guarantee a return on shareholder investment while making sure the rest of us feel ugly and inadequate. Fame-hungry singers are forced to ape a tired formula where they must breathlessly over-emote and wantonly gyrate their way to the top of the charts. Much of the music industry has become little more than a voyeuristic platform where botox-overloaded, butt-implanted dancers display their wares while mouthing along to digitally enhanced backing tracks.

Across the TV and film worlds, producers have been engaged in a cynical race to the bottom of the cultural barrel. While there are still pockets of thought-provoking material out there, much of what is fed to us via the mainstream is no more than a noisy assault on the senses and an insult to our intelligence. In a bid for our increasingly jaded attention, ratings-obsessed executives try to appeal to our baser instincts by inviting us to revel in sensationalism designed to disrupt and unnerve. Many big-budget movies are bombastic, frenetically edited and peppered with explosions, expletives and deafening, narrative-free conflict that tells audiences nothing about the human condition and everything about the bottom line. Triviality is the order of the day on primetime TV, where producers tend to patronise and talk down to us while ignoring a duty to entertain, educate and inform. Grotesque look-at-me caricatures compete in cynical, pointlessly shocking scenarios designed to denigrate and humiliate participants and audiences alike. Bland, formulaic shows in which ordinary members of the public compete in tortuously manufactured dancing, singing and baking competitions dominate the schedules. During weeks of interminable knockout rounds designed to shame losers and keep advertisers happy, hyped-up studio audiences whoop and cheer at anything that is put in front of them, undermining the notion of discernment and meaningful appreciation. These same tired formulas are then endlessly repackaged using minor celebrities in place of ordinary punters, in the hope that semi-recognisable nobodies feigning shock, surprise and carefully choreographed breakdowns will add some much-needed spice to the proceedings. Energy levels throughout these tawdry offerings must be kept at hysterical levels to hide an absence of meaning.

Post-watershed, the mainstream channels mostly rely on preening panel-show contestants fresh from the comedy circuit competing in asinine quiz shows designed to virtue signal fashionably orthodox political opinions while attempting to demoralise audiences with laddish innuendo and sneeringly ironic humour.

Across mainstream news networks hyperbole and partisanship have become endemic as producers desperately try to keep audiences anxiously engaged. Every news story must be 'unprecedented', every environmental report a 'catastrophe', every change of opinion a 'worrying U-turn'. No longer seen as a vehicle for well-informed enquiry, interviews with politicians have become an excuse for ridicule and 'gotcha moments' that play well on social media. Similarly, current-affairs shows thrive on incivility, whipped-up conflict and manufactured grievance. Self-serving politicians bolster technocratic, managerial oligarchs who bolster the media who bolster politicians who bolster the technocrats and round they go, all the while forgetting about their primary duty to keep the public informed.

In TV-land everything must either be 'super exciting' or 'utterly appalling'. Nuance, quiet contemplation and deep intellectual enquiry are mistakenly assumed to be ratings losers. There are some notable exceptions, of course. Smaller channels such as BBC Four and Sky Arts have a wealth of fascinating content, while Channel Four and Sky One air daily repeats of classic *The Simpsons* episodes. Anyone looking for insights into the human condition, as well as useful tips on how to live a meaningful life, should pay particular attention to the first ten seasons of this remarkable series, first aired in December 1989. Each one of the 226 episodes is packed with deep philosophical musings, hilarious social commentary and razor-sharp satire. Despite their many flaws, the adorably dysfunctional Simpson family always manages to redeem itself through good humour, kindness and common sense. Throughout their many trials and tribulations, they remain a devoted family with a strong moral ethos. Elsewhere in the series, cleverly conceived archetypes are put through their paces so that we might understand our own failings and pomposities a little better. Each beautifully written episode is a parable on human folly and the healing power of redemption. In season seven, episode four, for instance, ten-year-old Bart decides to sell his soul to best friend Milhouse only to discover that a soul-free existence isn't worth living. Creator Matt Groening cites this particular episode as one of his favourites; it has even been used as a teaching aid in secondary-school religious-studies classes. These classic episodes never lose their sheen and benefit from repeated viewings. All human life is there. You may want to turn to them whenever you seek solace.

Notwithstanding these notable exceptions, what we are left with in all of this is a perpetual, competitive yelling into the void. In all the noisy hyperbole and wilful obfuscation, ordinary people are at a loss as to know where to turn or what to believe. In order to liberate ourselves from crippling convention and dull decencies, we are being encouraged to embrace chaos, vulgarity and meaninglessness. Traditional values and cultural norms must be challenged in the name of progress, and yet no hope of redemption is forthcoming. Life is crude and ugly, the mainstream appears to be telling us, so why not revel in the debauchery and to hell with the consequences.

This coarsening of our culture has left many young men feeling profoundly demoralised and sapped of hope. Where once they picked up a book, learnt a new skill or listened to music, young people are now being bombarded with the screeching narcissism of celebrities and hollow social-media platforms, where reasoned argument is replaced by text-based assertion. Instead of lifting us out of our malaise, mainstream popular culture encourages us to turn inward and revel in ugliness and despair. Titillation, mockery and prurience have come to define a culture that feeds off the needy and preys on the vulnerable.

We must therefore be vigilant and resist the lure of the gutter and the sneer of the nihilist. There is beauty and trans-cendence beyond the trashy mainstream, and we must devote our time to seeking out the truth. The late philosopher Sir Roger Scruton describes beauty as something we 'feel at home with', something we can feel a part of, something that 'invites us in and welcomes us'.[14]

Steer adolescent minds away from the mindless frippery of the mainstream and from those who seek to desecrate the sacred and the beautiful. Make sure your child is made aware of their rich cultural heritage and imbue them with hope, possibility and above all gratitude.

A note from Sir Roger Scruton

'We have a duty to find the things we love and the best way to do that is to look at what other people have loved. And that's what culture is, the reside of everything that those who came before us thought worthwhile to preserve.'[15]

The wonders of new media

The mainstream may have largely abandoned its remit to inform, educate and entertain, but meaningful content has never been more plentiful or accessible if you know where to look. Beyond the shallow confines of social media, pornography and funny animal videos, the internet offers a vast treasure trove of informative, educational and entertaining content. Forget about mainstream media's schedule-restricted sound-bite culture and immerse yourself in thousands of hours of unrestricted long-form discussion forums with some of today's sharpest minds and enjoy a vast archive of material featuring some of the world's greatest thinkers.

Discover free podcasts created by passionate communicators keen to share big ideas and debate important issues. For a small monthly subscription fee, you can access a vast library of audiobooks from classic literary fiction to the latest blockbusters.

The literary world can be daunting, so here are some classics you might have never got around to reading. Each one of these books contains profound truths about the human condition:

War and Peace/Anna Karenina – Leo Tolstoy

The Mill on the Floss – George Eliot

Jude the Obscure – Thomas Hardy

Revolutionary Road – Richard Yates

Darkness Visible – William Styron

1984/The Road to Wigan Pier/Animal Farm –
George Orwell

A Grief Observed/The Lion, the Witch and the Wardrobe –
C. S. Lewis

The Catcher in the Rye – J. D. Salinger

The Grapes of Wrath – John Steinbeck

Frankenstein – Mary Shelley

The World As Will and Idea – Arthur Schopenhauer

Notes from the Underground – Fydor Dostoyevsky

Identity – Francis Fukuyama

The Portrait of a Lady – Henry James

Don't forget to read the great poets (such as John Milton, Lord Byron, John Wordsworth and Philip Larkin) too.

Head to YouTube and discover a rich seam of long-form debate, documentaries and lectures covering a diversity of topics. Here are just a few forums you might want to explore:

Modern Philosophy In this series of forty-five-minute programmes from the 1970s and '80s, Professor Bryan Magee interviews some of the greatest thinkers and writers of the twentieth century, including Herbert Marcuse, Iris Murdoch and Noam Chomsky. There is a particularly illuminating interview with Isaiah Berlin on why philosophy matters. Ignore the cheesy '70s clothes and backdrop.

Oxford and Cambridge Unions Our greatest universities offer a series of lively cultural, social and political debates covering a diverse range of topics from whether socialism works to the role of the media in a post-truth age.

Intelligence Squared Features a raft of discussions and debates on a range of subjects from the Catholic church to capitalism.

Munk Debates Attracts the brightest thinkers of our time to weigh in on all the big issues of the day. The biannual debates have included such luminaries as Henry Kissinger, Stephen Fry, Paul Krugman, Fareed Zakaria, Tony Blair, Christopher Hitchens and Jordan Peterson.

Uncommon Knowledge A web series in which political leaders, scholars, journalists and today's big thinkers share their views with veteran author and research fellow Peter Robinson. Topics include everything from how to bring up boys to empowering students.

The New Culture Forum Politician, author and journalist Peter Whittle introduces long-form cultural, political and philosophical discussions with leading figures of the day. Topics include the gender war and political correctness with guests such as writer Lionel Shriver and the late philosopher Sir Roger Scruton.

TED The TED media organisation prides itself on having 'ideas worth spreading'. These pithy talks of no more than eighteen minutes can be enjoyed by anyone seeking 'a deeper understanding of the world'. The site includes more than 2,600 lectures from world-renowned figures such as Bill Gates and

Michelle Obama to more intimate exchanges by experts in a particular field.

The Rubin Report Ex-comedian Dave Rubin in long-form discussion with controversial thinkers such as Douglas Murray and Bret Weinstein. Covers a wide range of topics from toxic masculinity and patriarchy to atheism and the new liberal elite.

Joe Rogan Show Relaxed but insightful discussions between world-renowned comic Joe Rogan and prominent media commentators and thinkers.

The Festival of Ideas Annual event promoting free speech and the sharing of controversial ideas filmed in front of a live audience.

Rebel Wisdom Long-form discussion forum exploring issues around spirituality and culture – check out Ken Wilber discussing 'The Intellectual Dark Web and Integrated Stages of Development'. Rebel Wisdom also organise 'New Masculinity Retreats', offering 'psychological and meditative techniques' that take men on a journey of self-exploration.

TRIGGERnometry Comedians Konstantin Kisin and Francis Foster host in-depth discussions about issues of the day from woke culture to ideas around forgiveness.

The Art of Manliness Discussion forum featuring subjects that directly affect men.

Conversations with John Anderson Former Australian deputy prime minister is joined by some of the world's foremost thought leaders to discuss the cultural, political and social landscape. Subjects include the crisis of meaning, the undermining of Western civilisation and the importance of trust in a civil society.

Spiked Robust political and cultural discussions around issues of the day.

Harbouring respect for elders and those in authority

Make sure your son respects adults and listens to their advice. Remind him that wisdom comes with age and that he can learn a lot from older people. Demonstrate your own authority by guiding him down a righteous path.

Being true to himself

In order to be true to himself, your son needs to be comfortable in his own skin. This is a lifelong quest, but the sooner he starts to examine what motivates him, the more he will discover what gives his life meaning. Finding his authentic voice will be one of Act Two's biggest achievements.

Teach your adolescent son about the importance of:

- Seeking out healthy role models
- Setting clear boundaries
- Avoiding aggressive, ugly music
- Treating everyone with respect
- Not following the herd
- Standing up to bullies

A note on puberty — some fatherly advice

Dealing with insecurity You may feel awkward about the way you look or that other people are judging you unfairly, but it is important to remember that everyone feels self-conscious, especially around strangers. Even confident adults worry about what other people think of them. You want to be liked but feel unlikeable and therefore unworthy of people's respect, so you make up stories in your head about how weird you are. Your lack of self-confidence becomes a self-fulfilling prophecy. So, next time you feel awkward in a crowded room remember that everyone else is telling themselves the same negative story. We are all nervous, vulnerable creatures seeking connection, so try not to feel too isolated.

Coming to terms with physical changes Between the age of ten and sixteen, you will undergo a dramatic physical transformation. As you move from childhood to adulthood, be prepared for growth spurts, maturing genitals and a deepening voice. These changes can be profoundly disorientating as you and your body struggle to adapt to a new mode of being. Remember, those spots on your face and that anxious knot in the stomach are all part of the growing-up process, so try not to despair.

Being yourself around girls It's a sad irony that puberty and sexual awakening hit us just when we are feeling at our least attractive. Girls mature faster than boys, so try not to take their indifference to heart. Once you hit sexual maturity and your body has made all the necessary adjustments, women will start to notice you, and you'll know for sure that you have become a fully functioning man.

Developing a personality Get to know yourself even though you may feel awkward in your skin. Understanding what makes you tick is a great confidence builder. The more you allow yourself to develop, the less awkward you will feel. Don't berate yourself for making mistakes – you are still learning – and try to trust your instincts; they are usually right.

Realising you are not the only one You may feel your parents don't understand you and that the rest of the world is blind to your needs. This is just a natural reaction to all those profound physical and psychological changes. Feelings of isolation will fade once you have matured.

Making friends and keeping them Lifelong friendships are often forged during adolescence, so choose your friends wisely. Try to hang out with kind, intelligent people with a keen sense of humour and a love of the absurd (a sure sign of acumen). Avoid cynics, bores and haters.

Adolescence – in summary

- Be vulnerable but don't be weakened by your vulnerability

- Avoid self-pity

- Turn your back on coarse popular culture

- Be your own man and don't follow the herd

- Delayed gratifications are more meaningful

- Respect our history, culture and Christian heritage (even if you are not religious)

- Avoid shallow pleasures

- Celebrate hundreds of years of Western culture with a grand tour of some of Europe's greatest cities, including Florence, Rome, Venice and Vienna

- Find meaning in long-form debates and discussions online, and avoid noisy, shallow mainstream media

- Stay away from addictive, stress-inducing social media

- Learn to think for yourself at university, and value the importance of free speech and open debate

- Read or listen to the great works of fiction

- Watch the first ten seasons of *The Simpsons* for valuable insights into how to live a meaningful life – return to them whenever you seek wisdom or solace

- Listen respectfully to those with opposing views and don't shut down people you disagree with

- Show humility and expect to have your opinions challenged – remember, you don't always have to be right

Act Three
Relationships and Parenthood

Sighing like furnace, with a woeful ballad
made to his mistress' eyebrow

With the vagaries of puberty behind us, the task of becoming a fully fledged adult can begin in earnest. By the time we reach our late teens, a certain amount of levelling up will have occurred. Boys are no longer lagging behind girls when it comes to physical and mental maturity.

As earnest young men, we start to embrace the idea of independence by moving out of the parental home, attending higher education or apprentice schemes, finding work and embarking on more serious long-term relationships. With women no longer seen as distant and unknowable, the sexes start to come together as equals, although a reluctance to settle down allows us time to experiment with our sexuality and discover what it means to be intimate with another human being.

In our late twenties and early thirties, we hit a crossroads. Deciding whether to continue playing the field or find someone with whom to spend the rest of your life is one of the most important decisions you will ever have to make. By now, many single women will have become acutely aware of their ticking biological clock, so wanting to keep your options open may come into direct conflict with her need to start a family, although the long-standing social contract between men and women is shifting as both sexes choose to delay getting married.

In 1846, the average age of marriage for women was 24.7 and 25.7 for men. Since the 1970s, that average has been steadily rising. According to the Office for National Statistics, by 1999 the age at which men got married had risen to over thirty. This milestone didn't happen for women until 2010. The ONS figures for 2017 show the average age had jumped to 38 for men and 35.7 for women.[1] If this trend continues, it could have profound implications for the future of traditional family life.

According to the British Fertility Society, a woman's ability to reproduce starts to decline dramatically in her mid thirties, decreasing year on year, regardless of health and fitness.[2] Most girls are born with around two million eggs. By adolescence, however, that number has dropped to around 400,000. At age thirty-seven, only about 25,000 remain, by which time the quality of the eggs will have declined significantly.

From about the age of thirty, a man's testosterone level also begins to fall by approximately 2 per cent a year according to official NHS figures.[3] This drop in the male sex hormone is often accompanied by a declining libido. As a result, conceiving becomes less likely with each passing year.

Realising that meaningful relationships take time to develop, many single women in their mid thirties, possibly with full-time careers, may decide to give up on the idea of finding 'the one' in favour of going it alone, either with the help of a sperm donor or through an adoption agency. As a single man approaching middle age, you too will have to make a pragmatic decision about the sort of future you want for yourself.

Our longing for intimacy, security and romantic love can often come into conflict with that niggling biological need to spread our seed far and wide. While we should always aim to keep love and sex mutually inclusive, both of these powerful drives can exist in isolation, so it's important to be aware of the hold they can exert over us.

Falling in love has always been a heady if risky affair. Our yearning for meaningful connection is tempered by a fear of rejection and loss of freedom, a dichotomy that can leave us wary of commitment. Making ourselves vulnerable to another human being can seem at odds with our instinct for survival. A growing army of men is turning its back on women altogether. 'Men Going Their Own Way', or MGTOWs, for instance, fear that relationships are tilted in women's favour and that the cards are stacked against men when it comes to divorce settlements and child-custody battles. Another online movement known as Involuntary Celibates, or INCELS, feel aggrieved by their inability to attract a mate and thus take their resentments out on women.

These may be extreme cases, but the fact that groups such as MGTOW even exist speaks of a growing reluctance amongst ordinary men to enter into committed long-term relationships. Our need for connection set against a longing to be free can seem especially poignant in Act Three when we have to make important decisions about the future. Friends will have started to pair off, and you may worry about ending up alone. With so much riding on your decision, choosing to spend the rest of your life with someone can seem a daunting prospect. Unrealistic expectations, a lack of moral certainty, concerns about rising divorce rates and post-Me Too paranoia only adds to our sense of anxiety.

As men, we have a tendency to indulge in fantasies we know are bad for us – the lure of unlimited sexual conquests, of living without consequences, of having our cake and eating it. We long to be free of inhibitions, of responsibilities and of not having to defer to anyone but ourselves. We imagine a utopian world in which we never have to grow up or settle down, never have to grow old or die. And yet we know in our hearts that we cannot live a meaningful life without sacrificing these selfish desires.

Our dogged belief in fantasy can make reality seem dreary by comparison. Only by accepting life's harsher realities can we begin to make sense of the hand we have been dealt. We all of us yearn to find meaning and connection, but it's important to remember that we cannot have one without the other. We live in disconnected, nomadic times, where the young move to cities, the elderly languish in care homes and the classes fail to integrate. This lack of community cohesion feeds our longing to feel settled. Finding stillness and a rooted place to call home gives us the opportunity to build the kind of deep connections that mitigate our own failures and disappointments, giving us that sense of belonging we crave. 'Dwelling in the land', as philosopher Martin Heidegger put it, allows us to stand back and be at one with the world. Once we have found that solid foundation and sense of shared responsibility, we are in a much better position to deal with setbacks.

Of course, fantasising is a natural response to the limitations life imposes on us, but in our all-you-can-eat culture, the line between fantasy and reality has become increasingly blurred. Unrestrained personal fulfilment is seen as a goal worth pursuing. We start to buy into the lie. Suddenly our fantasies don't seem so fantastical any more. Why shouldn't we sleep around if it makes us feel good? Who needs to be tied down by a wife and family? We think we have a right to be happy and that happiness is a goal in itself rather than a consequence of a life well lived. And so we abandon our search for meaning and embrace shallow, fickle pleasures only to discover that they leave us feeling even more bereft. The promise of fulfilment is always just out of reach; connections are tenuous, pleasures short-lived and meaning almost impossible to find. If we are serious about living a meaningful life, we must let go of youthful folly and embrace the wisdom of maturity.

Whenever you feel the lure of unhealthy temptations, take a step back and consider your future. Do you really want to be the sort of man who is blown about by casual whims and desires, or would you prefer to take control of your life and make grown-up decisions based on long-term considerations?

Finding love

If you are struggling to find someone to share your life with, it's easy to start blaming yourself – if only you were richer, taller, cleverer. You look around at your happily settled contemporaries and wonder what makes them so special. Why them and not you? The truth is we have no real control over who we find connection with. Our love lives depend almost entirely on happenstance. Nearly all future connections will depend on decisions taken now. The film *Sliding Doors* perfectly encapsulates this rather poignant truth about human relationships. The story imagines two scenarios: in the first, we see a young woman played by Gwyneth Paltrow missing her train and in so doing missing out on meeting the love of her life; in the second, we witness what might have happened in a parallel universe had the woman managed to board the train and meet the man of her dreams.[4]

Every day we cross paths with people we never actually meet, who might have turned out to have been a lifelong friend or lover – the fleeting glance of a stranger passing you in the street, that friend of a friend you were never formally introduced to at a party. Life is full of unrealised possibilities, so if you are feeling frustrated by the lack of love in your life, remember it's no one's fault if the stars have yet to align.

All's fair . . .

While it's important to remain open to the possibility of love, at times it can feel as though you are trapped inside a bloody bear pit, where the winners take all the spoils. If you are already feeling vulnerable and unsure of yourself, the modern dating scene, with its callous swiping, easy dismissals and infinite choice, can seem positively Darwinian. Although you should never give up hope of finding someone, you may want to consider why you are struggling to connect in the real world. Consider how you come across to the opposite sex. Perhaps you are attracted to a work colleague but feel frustrated because she never seems to notice you. Rather than feeling angry and embittered, reflect on whether her lack of interest is down to your attitude. Perhaps you come across as needy, whiny or arrogant; remember she can only judge you according to what she finds. Try to see yourself as others see you. Are you the sort of person *you* would choose to have as a friend or lover? If not, think about how you might become more affable and less resentful. Try to remain open-minded and generous of spirit.

The popularity of online dating apps has seen a revolution in the way we connect. Women no longer have to rely on men to make the first move, which for many women has come as a source of relief, the consensus being that men can be pretty hopeless when it comes to asking them out. This democratisation of dating has also come as a boon to men who may have grown weary of always having to be the instigator. Contrary to popular belief, not all men enjoy the thrill of the chase. Many of us find the whole courtship ritual either deeply embarrassing or impossible to fathom. Going up to strangers in bars and asking them fatuous questions about whether they like going to bars doesn't sit well, especially now that Weinstein and others like him have tainted the whole idea of the male pursuit.

The online world appears to offer us a less self-conscious way to meet, as well as the thrill of unlimited opportunities, but this is all an illusion. The truth is, our ability to make decisions is dependent on our willingness to accept compromise. Too much choice feeds our indecision and makes having to choose even more stressful. You may balk at the idea of sacrifice, but whether you realise it or not, every encounter involves a certain degree of give and take. Are you prepared, for instance, to sacrifice a pretty face for a witty sense of humour? Will the joy of a younger woman's boundless energy outweigh your different perspectives on life? Does kindness compensate for crooked teeth and a deafening laugh? Some of these compromises may seem trivial or even cruel, but they all feed into our decision to be with someone.

Rather than leaving it to chance, you may find it helpful to write a list of all your needs and desires in order of priority, bearing in mind that there will always be X-factors at play. When compiling your list, try to distinguish between shallow desire and deeper yearnings. Physical attraction may be an important factor, but don't allow a pretty face to cloud your judgement when choosing a long-term partner. As men, we can be easily swayed by outward appearances (evolutionary biologists have shown that a pleasing appearance signifies good physical and mental health), but we shouldn't assume that an attractive face comes with a personality to match.[5] Looks can be horribly deceiving, so try to see beyond physical attraction to the complex person beneath. If you are hoping to settle down, your chosen mate will need more than a great figure and a sexy smile to hold your interest.

As with so much of the online world, digital dating can become highly additive – with each swipe, the hope of someone prettier, younger, funnier, better. Our hunger for perfection makes us less willing to take a chance and meet in the real world. Each failed attempt at a connection weakens our resolve, sapping our spirits and damaging our self-esteem. We start to question our judgement and faith in humanity. The world appears to be full of stupid, unattractive people who consistently fail to live up to our exacting standards.

In short, internet dating can feed unrealistic expectations and narcissistic tendencies, so make sure you explore all other options before signing up. Here are a few less demoralising ways to meet potential partners.

- Work romances can be tricky if you share the same office space, so if you work in a large organisation, try expanding your circle of connections beyond your immediate department. Many successful relationships begin at work, so remain open-minded to the possibility.

- Throw regular dinner parties and ask friends to bring along interesting new people. If you all get along, then chances are they will ask you to one of their dinner parties, thereby expanding your circle of friends and the potential for deeper, more intimate connections.

- Join a sports or book club where you will meet like-minded people.

- Take up a hobby and attend evening classes.

- Be gregarious. Even if you feel like staying home, always take up invitations from friends and acquaintances. You will usually enjoy yourself once you get there, and you never know who you might meet.

- Be engaged. The more interested you are in other people the more they will gravitate towards you. Don't wait for anybody else to make the first move. Be brave, dive in and know that we are all hungry for human interaction.

Before even attempting a romantic connection, ask two simple but profound questions:

- What do I actually want from a relationship?

- How far am I prepared to compromise in order to get what I want?

It is essential at this stage to understand your motivations. So why *are* you looking to start a relationship (be honest)?

- Are you lonely?

- Are you horny?

- Are you ready to settle down and have a family?

- Are you a serial monogamist?

- Are you looking for company and a bit of fun?

- Are you frightened of being alone?

- Do you worry about being left on the shelf?

- Are you panicking about your age?

- Are you wanting someone to look after you?

- Are you anxiously comparing yourself to happily married friends?

- Are you looking for a companion more than a lover?

- Are you desperate to have kids but not necessarily a relationship?

- Are you wanting to please your parents?

- Is convention forcing you to 'do the right thing'?

- Are you looking for affirmation and personal gratification?

- Do you want to settle down and have kids with a woman you love?

Be aware that there is no such thing as Mr or Mrs 'Right'. It is a myth perpetuated by fiction writers and advertisers. We are all a complicated mix of fears, hopes, dreams, disappointments, expectations, ambitions, weird obsessions and existential longings.

The more you chase after simplistic notions such as finding 'the one' the more you lose sight of life's complexities. Get on with the rest of your life and allow connections to occur naturally – love often appears when we are least expecting it.

Before entering into a relationship, it's also vitally important that you get to know yourself. Be honest about your needs and intentions from the start so that nobody gets hurt. If there is someone you are interested in, give them a chance and remember that perfection is for the gods. All human beings are flawed, and that includes you – it's what makes us human. Remind yourself of this humbling fact every day. Write 'PERFECTION DOES NOT EXIST' in big capital letters on a Post-it Note and stick it next to your computer. Before going on a date, look in the mirror and repeat the phrase half a dozen times, remembering your own shortcomings. Reining in expectations will free you from the tyranny of entitlement and false hope. By accepting that we live in an imperfect world populated by flawed individuals we can start to empathise and view each other not as a threat but as fellow imperfect travellers on the rocky road to meaning. With expectations tempered, you will become less judgemental and more willing to give others the benefit of the doubt. Letting go of perfection will open you up to the possibility of love. If you are still struggling to form intimate relationships, book some sessions with a psychotherapist. You might discover there are unresolved traumas blocking your ability to let go.

Dating may have become more democratised in the digital age, but the fear of rejection still hangs over us, even in Act Three. Take comfort in the knowledge that we all suffer from the same abandonment issues embedded in us from the moment we leave our mothers' wombs. Men are deeply sensitive souls at heart

– look at all our great romantic poets and songwriters – but we sometimes struggle to translate that inner profundity into outward expressions of desire. We like to think of ourselves as smooth-operating George Clooney types or swaggeringly romantic Rudolph Valentinos but often end up feeling more like Austin Powers doing that embarrassing dance routine. The idea that we are part of a post-Weinstein 'rape culture' has only intensified our fear of appearing predatory. We may think we are in control of our romantic destiny, but according to clinical psychologist Dr Stephen Blumenthal, when it comes to choosing a mate, women hold all the power. So, if you've found someone you like, be confident, kind and engaging; be all these things and more, but remember, she will have the final say on whether you spend the rest of your life together. Don't despair if she rejects you sexually; not all attraction is carnal, and you may end up having a deeply meaningful platonic friendship.

A note on imperfection

Imagine how dull life would be if we were all perfect. Your unique quirks, mad eccentricities and strange foibles are what make you loveable. A meaningful life can only begin once we accept that we are all deeply flawed individuals with huge amounts of potential and the capacity for change.

Dating – A couple of dos and don'ts

Should you pay for dates? Now that men and women are supposedly equal, the question of who pays for what can become complicated if we're not careful. Traditionally, women expected to be wooed before succumbing to men's amorous advances. Paying for flowers and nights out proved we were serious. Nowadays no one is quite sure whether these unspoken rules still apply. According to *Debrett's Guide for the Modern Gentleman,* 'the person who requests the pleasure, pays for the pleasure'.[6] With that in mind, why not show her your thoughtful side by paying for dates, especially during the courting process. She will want to know that you are generous and solvent (important considerations when seeking a possible father for her children). Be aware, however, that some women might see your eagerness to foot the bill as patronising or even misogynistic, the assumption being that women can't afford to pay or that by paying you, the man, are expecting something in return. To avoid any confusion perhaps the fairest solution is for you to split all bills down the middle. Be aware, however, that there is nothing women hate more than stinginess in men. If you are genuinely struggling financially, why not buy your date silly but thoughtful gifts instead of paying for expensive meals. Presents feel less like a transaction and more like a genuine expression of your affection.

Should you be chivalrous? Many women feel conflicted about male chivalry. Some see it as a paternalistic anathema from a bygone era when women were referred to as 'wenches' and men stomped around in metal suits killing each other with axes. For others, the word conjures up romantic knights in shining armour galloping across misty fields to rescue distressed damsels.

In reality, being chivalrous just means treating women with respect. In these egalitarian times, perhaps we should broaden chivalry's remit to include showing respect for all human beings, regardless of gender.

Here are a few acts of chivalry we could all adopt to make other people's lives better:

- Always hold doors open for people and let them walk through first.

- On public transport give up your seat to someone who might need it more than you.

- Open the car door for your passenger.

- If there are two of you walking along the street, offer to take the outside of the pavement.

- If a friend is feeling chilly, offer them your jacket. Selflessness is one of our most attractive, life-affirming traits.

- Always call when you say you are going to – reliability makes other people feel respected.

- At dinner parties, pull out the chair for the person next to you, whether you know them or not.

- Be the one to fill the car with petrol and always err on the side of generosity.

- After a night out with a friend, send them a text to check they got home safely.

- Compliment your friends and tell them how well they look. Remind your wife how beautiful/funny/intelligent/silly she is and how much you appreciate all she does for you. Tell friends and family how much you love them, and demonstrate your love with words of affirmation and the occasional hug. Even strangers will appreciate a genuine compliment – if you like the look of someone's jacket, tell them how much it suits them. Ask them where they bought it and admire the quality of the stitching. Be effusive and engaging if they crack a joke or compliment you back. Humans love nothing more than receiving compliments, so imagine how agreeable life would be if we all expressed our admiration for each other a bit more.

- Flowers aren't just for women. Why not send your best friend a bouquet next time he is feeling depressed?

- Brighten someone's day by writing them an old-fashioned letter.

- Be polite to strangers and treat everyone you meet the way you would like to be treated.

- If a friend or family member is going through a traumatic break-up, go round to their house with a bottle of wine and offer them a shoulder to cry on.

- Give whomever you are speaking to your undivided attention. Try not to be distracted by what's going on in the background. If someone is choosing to spend time with you, make it count.

Pornography – the dangers

Whenever we feel lonely, frustrated or dejected, it's tempting to turn to pornography in the hope that the sight of other people being intimate with each other will alleviate the pain. For most of us, however, porn is little more than a dispiriting exercise in itch-scratching and a lousy substitute for meaningful connection. What dribble of pleasure there is tends to be fleeting, messy and mired in self-disgust. A few minutes or hours later and the itch is back. According to Dr Stephen Blumenthal, who has worked extensively in men's mental health, for a growing minority of users, porn's unrequited promises are becoming a horrifying addiction, leading to dysfunctional sex lives, broken relationships, depression and even suicide. None of which is conducive to a meaningful life.

Clinical psychologist Heather Wood has made a special study of internet porn and believes that in some cases pornography may be used to 'elaborate or amplify already deviant sexual interests'.[7] Of course, not everyone who watches porn goes on to develop mental-health issues or deviant sexual practices, but the evidence of harm shouldn't be ignored.

Those who have used online pornography for any length of time say that the material loses its potency with repeated viewing. Desensitisation soon kicks in; perverse or degrading acts become normalised. Cynical pornographers know that in order to hold on to their customers they must keep dopamine levels firing on all cylinders, which means offering ever more extreme material. Scenes of sadomasochism have become almost de rigueur in even the most pedestrian porn clips. One thing you will rarely if ever see in pornographic movies is a couple making love in the missionary position while gazing longingly into each other's eyes – it seems real intimacy and meaningful connection doesn't play well with desensitised viewers.

So why should we be concerned about pornography's increasing reliance on ever more extreme and depraved content? Well, for those dealing with the fallout, such as Dr Blumenthal, porn consumption has become a ticking time bomb: 'I am seeing more and more males habitually seeking out ever more disturbing sexual imagery. It is distorting their minds and making them seriously depressed.' And it isn't just awkward adolescents who are having their minds and sex drives unalterably rewired. Middle-aged men are turning to porn in increasingly large numbers, either to spice up waning sex lives or as an easy substitute for the real thing. Although men have always sought sexual distractions, Dr Blumenthal believes the ubiquity of internet porn is feeding addictive behaviour. A 2014 Cambridge University study found that pornography triggers brain activity in sex addicts in much the same way that drugs trigger drug addicts.[8]

Before the internet, mainstream porn was limited to cheesy top-shelf magazines with titles such as *High Society*, *Razzle* and *Playboy*. The garishly lit double-page spreads of pimply, bubble-permed 'models' sprawled across nastily fibred rugs in grim provincial backrooms seem almost quaint compared with today's high-definition clips of perfectly preened 'adult entertainment stars' getting it on in honey-lit Hollywood mansions. Back in the 1970s and '80s, publishers of 'dirty mags' even felt obliged to include sexy photographs of speedboats and Ferraris simply to break up the tedium. Yes, there were hardcore videos out there, but only if you were prepared to get your hands dirty browsing the unhygienic shelves of dank, Soho sex shops. But even then, the gaudy covers and titillating titles – *Jet Sex*, *Up and Coming* and *Cinderotica* spring depressingly to mind – gave little indication as to what was actually inside. Being ripped off came with the territory. An hour's worth of material might set you back thirty quid but with much of the content consisting of excruciatingly dull, appallingly acted filler. Refunds of course were out of the question.

Before we were able to swipe our way to instant sexual gratification, tastes were governed by what was available and the effort and expense of acquiring it. Fine if you happened to be into bubble-permed girl-on-rug action; for everyone else, it was a case of using your imagination and hoping for the best. The internet has expanded our arousal horizons exponentially, providing a platform for every sexual proclivity imaginable (and many more besides). Young men no longer have to worry about what other people might think (porn-mag purchases often came with a discreet brown paper bag). Today there are no limits and no judgements – just you, your screen and a virtual button to anywhere. But the consequences of so much unregulated freedom is only now becoming clear. And it is doctors like Blumenthal who are having to pick up the pieces. He worries about the long-term impact on men's mental and emotional well-being: 'Humans have the capacity for rational, deliberating thought, but we are also impulse driven. When it comes to porn's ease of access and the anonymity of being online, we are often powerless to say no, and that can lead men to some very unedifying places, compounding feelings of shame and self-loathing.'

More worryingly, pornography intrudes on our relationships and our capacity to form them, says Blumenthal. It has become like a retreat from the real world, an uncomplicated, non-judgemental, private place where insecure young men indulge fantasies and hide from their worries and anxieties. In Act Four, older men will often turn to pornography in times of crisis, during marital problems, for instance, or when they feel lonely and afraid. For many men, porn acts as a kind of anti-depressant, but according to Blumenthal, all that unattainable imagery only exacerbates feelings of isolation.

What is becoming abundantly clear is that action needs to be taken to protect the most vulnerable, and yet successive governments continue to scupper any meaningful regulation. Heather Wood believes that restricting availability and access is unrealistic and that there needs to be more awareness about the effects of internet porn on the unconscious mind.[9]

Dr Blumenthal thinks we need to go further and that the lack of effective regulation has been short-sighted and irresponsible in the extreme: 'A few years from now, we will look back and wonder what on earth we were thinking in much the same way we look back in disbelief at 1950s attitudes to smoking.' It is still unclear what the long-term health consequences might be; mainstream sites such as Pornhub and Brazzers are scarcely a decade old. But going on the evidence we have so far, Blumenthal believes monitoring users might be a useful first step in alleviating some of the shame and suffering he sees in his practice: 'Experience sampling is a highly reliable method of measuring how someone is feeling while they are engaged in online activities.' Indeed, Facebook have been using just such a method to monitor declines in subjective well-being experienced by social-media junkies. And it's relatively easy to implement: participants are sent text messages at random intervals throughout the day, with a link to an online survey. At the very least, this might provide some hard evidence, bringing all that private misery out into the open.

In the meantime, government should make it obligatory for every registered porn site to carry a prominent health warning, a bit like the ones used on cigarette packets. Instead of tar-encrusted lungs, the warning could feature a photograph of a lonely young man staring anxiously at a computer screen, underpants around his ankles. The wording might read something like this: *'DANGER – the site you are about to enter contains footage of actors engaging in fake sexual scenarios that bear little relationship to real life. Viewing such material can result in long-term damage to mental health, dissatisfaction, erectile dysfunction*, depression, anxiety and shame. Proceed with extreme caution.'*

A note on pornography

A 2016 analytics report of the website Pornhub revealed that in a single year its videos were watched 92 billion times by 64 million daily visitors; that works out at 12.5 videos for every person on the planet. It would take 524,641 years to watch all the clips back to back.

Fostering a healthy attitude to sex and relationships

As culture has coarsened so too has our attitude to sex. The proliferation of pornography is an obvious example, but even the mainstream media treats intercourse as little more than a smutty ratings winner. Their prurient obsession with sex speaks of a

---

* In 2014 NHS experts noted an increase in erectile dysfunction in otherwise healthy young men. They concluded that excessive porn use was the most likely factor at play.

broader disconnect between physical and emotional desire now permeating so much of our culture. When societies fixate on the mechanics of intercourse, it can be one portent of imminent collapse, as in the latter stages of the Roman Empire, the 'mauve' Oscar Wilde period at the end of the nineteenth century and the final few years of the Weimar Republic in Germany.[10]

One side effect of our moral laxity around sexual matters has been the failure to teach young men about the difference between shallow and deep connections. It's important therefore to keep reminding them that for sex to have any kind of meaning it must come from a place of love.

Don't build your house on sand

Attempting to maintain a relationship on the back of a drunken night of passion and some cute pillow talk can often be futile. Faced with shallow connections, it's important to know when to walk away so that you don't waste each other's time. Try not to hang around just because the sex was great. If left unchecked, sexual desire can end up owning you. Learn to tame your animal instincts and you will forge deeper, more long-lasting connections. Here are some positive character traits you might want to consider when choosing a life partner:

- Kindness

- Warmth

- Generosity

- A good listener

- Tenderness

- Humour
- A healthy sense of the absurd
- An adventurous spirit
- An ability to engage
- A willingness to laugh at herself
- Empathy
- Soulfulness
- Enthusiasm
- Authenticity
- Interest in other people
- Selflessness
- An ability to see the best in people
- A love of animals, music and art

Compatibility is essential, but so is patience. Sexual attraction can take time to develop, although many of us seem unwilling to wait. Our longing for intimacy means we are constantly on the lookout for easy connections, however inappropriate they may be. Perhaps you have found yourself fantasising about an attractive woman sitting opposite you on the train. Wondering whether she might be 'the one', you start to build a narrative based entirely on her physical appearance. She is no longer simply a fellow passenger but a goddess sent to save you from yourself. You sit there wondering whether to make your move. Your heartbeat quickens as you fantasise about a possible future together. What will your children look like? Should the two of you run away to Southern California and live by the ocean? You feel a warm glow of possibility. Have all the years of searching finally come to an end, right here on the grubby 5.45 to Manchester? You turn to ask for her number, but she's already alighted at Crewe.

Enjoy fantasising by all means, but don't expect miracles. Next time you berate yourself for your lack of courage, recognise when your mind is playing tricks and remember that meaningful relationships grow out of solid foundations.

Sex before marriage and cohabiting

When we are feeling unloved, casual sex can seem like a beguiling shortcut to the intimacy we crave. Promiscuity, however, is a poor substitute for monogamous love and usually leads to more loneliness and dissatisfaction. Jumping into bed on a first date may seem harmless but can often damage your chances of forming a deep and lasting connection.

We may snigger at the idea of having to leap through hoops to get what we want, but what previous generations understood, and what we tend to forget, is that sex doesn't happen in a vacuum. Those buttoned-up Victorians, for instance, were acutely aware that actions have consequences, and that sex and emotion are inextricably linked. For intercourse to mean more than just physical pleasure, it needs to happen within a clear moral and emotional framework. Understanding that sex is more than just recreational fun imbues romantic love with weight and profundity; the sanctified body is no longer simply a vessel for pleasure but a unifying bond that links the physical, spiritual and emotional realms.

Similarly, we tend to dismiss the 1940s and '50s as another stiflingly uptight period in our sexual history. Intercourse outside of marriage, for example, was still frowned upon, and one only has to consider the sexual modesty on display in films such as *Brief Encounter* to realise that sex wasn't something to be taken lightly.[11] But instead of sneering at their prudery, we should ask why a post-war generation viewed sex in this way. Maybe the spectre of all those wasted lives reminded them of the value of sexual intercourse's primary purpose, that of bringing life into the world. War had cheapened the very notion of human sanctity by sending thousands of young men off to die. Dignifying the means of creation reminded them that life mattered. Perhaps the high-minded morality of the post-war years was born out of a desire to find meaning in all the carnage. We haven't had to endure anything like the fallout of two world wars, so that fragile sense of our own mortality isn't there in quite the same way. The fact is, none of us would be here without that simple yet profound act of emotional and physical connection, so perhaps we should start treating sex with the respect it deserves.

On the tricky issue of whether we should delay sexual gratification, some argue that the only way for a relationship to develop fully is for a couple to engage in intercourse as quickly as possible once they start going out so as to avoid a build-up of sexual tension. The argument goes that once we have exposed ourselves physically, we are more inclined to reveal our authentic selves and thus be in a better position to judge whether or not to take the relationship further.

Others argue that relationships are cheapened when couples rush into sex. In a 2010 study, Professor Dean Busby from the School of Family Life at Brigham Young University attempted to find out what effect the timing of their first sexual encounter had on a couple's marriage. He surveyed more than 2,000 people aged from nineteen to seventy-one who had been married anywhere from six months to more than twenty years. The volunteers came from a variety of religious and secular backgrounds. When religiosity, length of relationship, income, education and race were taken into consideration, Busby found that couples who delayed sex within a relationship had better long-term prospects and greater overall satisfaction.

The benefits of waiting until marriage over having sex early on in a relationship were as follows:

- Relationships were 22 per cent more stable

- Couples were 20 per cent more satisfied with their relationship

- The quality of the sex was reported to be 15 per cent better

- Couples communicated 12 per cent better[12]

You should apply the same consideration to cohabiting. It's important to remember that dating and living together place very different demands on a relationship, so you need to think carefully before abandoning your independence. If money is tight, you may think it prudent to pool your resources in order to avoid having to pay two sets of rent. Perhaps you consider it foolhardy to marry someone without testing the water first. Statistics show, however, that cohabiting rarely leads to marriage[13] and doesn't always result in a long and happy life together. According to the ONS, the number of cohabiting couples continues to grow faster than married-couple and lone-parent families, with an increase of 25.8 per cent over the decade 2008 to 2018.[14]

You might think it outdated to be concerned about something as seemingly innocuous as living with someone you love, but a recent study by the *Journal of Marriage and Family* found that premarital cohabitation has short-term benefits but longer-term costs for marital stability. Couples who lived together before marriage had a lower divorce rate in their first year of marriage but a higher divorce rate after five years.[15] Lovers will often move in together for financial reasons – sharing accommodation keeps costs down – meaning that break-ups become a greater logistical challenge. Couples may wind up getting married even though that was never their original plan. This in turn can lead to a lower degree of marital satisfaction and a higher risk of divorce.

Celibacy and the meaningful life

Sometimes it can feel as though our biological urges are being manipulated and used against us in a cynical attempt to sell us stuff we don't need. Of course, sex has always been an effective selling tool, but a culture of hyper-sexuality has left many of us in a state of permanent anxiety. Are we getting enough? Are we acrobatic enough? Are we hot enough? Scantily clad models smoulder at us from giant billboards reminding us of what we can never have.

Sleeping with someone is no longer simply a fumbled expression of mutual attraction; it now comes with the added burden of expectation driven by airbrushed ideals, erotic fiction and always-up-for-it porn-star gymnastics. How can we, with our paunchy inadequacies, possibly keep up?

Authors such as E. L. James have opened a Pandora's box of sexual shenanigans previously the preserve of shady underground establishments.[16] The pressure to look, perform and, yes, dominate like Christian Grey has left many men feeling confused and inadequate. Just as desperate housewives are being encouraged to rise up and grab themselves a piece of the action, bewildered husbands are retreating to the less judgemental world of online porn.

We have all been sold a dirty-little sex lie, but instead of railing against the audacity of the deceit, we have become infatuated by the idea of carnal perfection. For women that means lusting after implausibly romantic, slightly dubious fictional hunks; for men, it means nothing less than uninhibited sex with super-model porn stars. We are now demanding to have our cynically imparted, hopelessly unrealistic fantasies fulfilled, and if partners fail to comply, then we will seek our pleasures elsewhere. Life is short, and we are 'worth it'.

So why should you consider embarking on a vow of celibacy? Perhaps you have recently emerged from a fraught relationship where sex had become a divisive issue. And now here you are, newly single, in a world of infinite sexual possibilities but without a roadmap. You could choose to dive headlong into this brave, new, uninhibited world, with all its promise of unfettered pleasures, but the sheer volume of sexual stimuli could soon become overwhelming. Sex in the media has become so joylessly ubiquitous that for many of us it feels pedestrian, tiresome almost. Everyone seems to be at it, but there are precious few ground rules, other than swiping left for 'no', or right for 'yes'.

Recreational copulation soon loses its appeal; we become satiated not only by the act itself but by the ugly, cynical industry that has grown up around it. Like the poor chocolate-factory worker who can no longer stand the taste of cocoa, we need time out in order to regain a sense of perspective. Try giving yourself a year off from sex, with the option to extend.

You should begin your bout of celibacy by turning down invitations from single male friends on the pull. Give your libido a break from the constant anxiety of desire. Avoiding the daily tidal wave of sexual imagery designed to set male minds racing will help but may prove tricky. If a billboard tries to seduce you into some pointless purchase with wanton, provocatively attired models, simply avert your gaze. Apply the same rule for shop windows and bus-shelter displays. Pouting sirens will be fighting for your attention on every street corner. Learning to blank out these stress-inducing images will be a useful first step in the purification of sexual desire.

Gawping at random women in the street is another challenge you will need to overcome. Even the most furtive glance can trigger sexual anxieties. That's not to say that when you emerge from exile you should stop admiring women. Indeed, we need to think hard about how we keep the flame of attraction burning. In the post-Me Too world, male sexuality has become a battleground of conflicting messages. We are told, for instance, that the 'male gaze' is inherently misogynistic, and yet society permits us free access to hardcore pornography, in which women are brutalised and treated as sex objects.

Human survival depends on our ability to express and act upon sexual desire within accepted parameters, but because of the shame around male sexuality those parameters have become blurred. We have reached a point where it is deemed acceptable for women to objectify men's bodies – as in *Fifty Shades of Grey*,

Poldark and all those commercials featuring bare-chested hunks – but sexist and inappropriate the other way around.

Because the sexual landscape is changing so fast, we need to have an honest debate about where the boundaries of acceptability now lie. All of us have a right to know where we stand on certain key issues. One woman's idea of flattery, for instance, may be another's idea of misogyny. This confusion around what is deemed acceptable came to a head in 2018 when 100 French women, including actress Catherine Deneuve, signed an opinion piece in *Le Monde* newspaper defending men's 'freedom to bother'.[17] The signatories acknowledged that while rape was indeed a crime and should be treated as such, 'hitting on someone insistently or awkwardly' is not an offence, nor is 'gallantry a chauvinist aggression'. If confusion around what is deemed acceptable is allowed to continue, what hope have we of moving on from the dysfunctions of the past? It's time we all had some clarity.

During your year of celibacy, think about how you might improve your attitude to women and sexuality. While it's important not to feel ashamed of your urges and to recognise that a healthy libido is something to celebrate, there are always improvements we can make when it comes to how we treat the opposite sex, both privately and in the public sphere. It might be something as simple as working on your chat-up lines, for example. During the sexual revolution of the 1960s and the decades that followed, men were often crude when it came to casual encounters with women. This may have been down to embarrassment; after all, we had only just emerged from the sexual austerity of the post-war years and were still coming to terms with the idea of liberation. Free from inhibitions, it was all too easy to pinch women's backsides or blurt out lewd or inappropriate comments without being fully aware of the consequences. Thankfully, many of those crass innuendoes that used to pepper men's speech have largely disappeared, but we should still be wary about falling into old pre-enlightenment ways, especially when we find ourselves in awkward or uncomfortable scenarios.

A period of hibernation will allow you to reconsider your approach to sex and relationships. Once you emerge, you will no longer feel the need to objectify women or to fall back on outdated macho posturing. The longer you remain without, the freer and wiser you will become – and remember this is only a temporary measure to bring meaning back to sexual intimacy. As that gnawing sense of lustful longing retreats, it can feel as though a hyperactive, burdensome adolescent has been unshackled from your side. You will start to realise just how much time you wasted thinking, worrying and obsessing about sex. Once you have made the decision to quit for a while, you will finally be free to focus on other more meaningful objectives. You could take up painting or learn to play the piano. Parties will no longer seem like breeding grounds of frustrated possibility and disappointment. If you need to let off steam, try going on a five-mile run or spend an hour in the gym.

After a while you might start to miss the intimacy of sex with someone you care about, but remember the trial is only temporary. When you do rejoin the land of the loving, you will feel purged and ready to begin anew.

If celibacy teaches us anything it is that we need to somehow tame our desires without killing them off completely. Allow yourself to be drawn in by the relentless tide of cheap sexual gimmickry and you risk being worn down by a gnawing sense of inadequacy. Going cold turkey, on the other hand, reminds us that beyond the easy thrill of the physical lies a deeper, more spiritual truth, rarely discussed by our infantile, sex–obsessed media. Whatever your sexual proclivities, we all of us need to set clear boundaries.

A note on gender stereotypes

Gender remains a confusing, topsy-turvy business, full of glaring contradictions and baffling misconceptions. We have been led to believe, for instance, that women are more emotionally connected than men, and yet so many love songs, philosophical works and romantic poems have been penned by males. Boys are supposed to be obsessed by sex, and yet it is girls who consume erotic fiction, swoon over the latest pop stars and spend hours in the bathroom trying to make themselves more alluring. The popularity of books such as *Fifty Shades of Grey* show that women still yearn for macho, bad-boy archetypes, even though 'traditional masculinity' is supposed to be bad for their health. Such graphic material is another example of how double standards have come to dominate the sexual conversation, allowing one set of rules for women and another for men. We are told that men are the dominant force in relationships, and yet the dynamic within many marriages would suggest otherwise. In many cases it is women rather than men who are the practical, down-to-earth decision makers and women who control much of the domestic sphere.

Fear of commitment

Are you holding out for the perfect partner? Do you prefer sexual freedom to a committed monogamous relationship? Playing the field and delaying marriage may have their appeal, but you need to think about the long-term consequences. When you do eventually decide to settle down, perhaps in your late thirties, forties or even fifties, the pool of potential partners will have shrunk considerably; remember that most women still get married in their mid thirties. This leaves you with two options: start dating much younger women and deal with all the uncertainty and changing priorities that come with fickle youth, or find yourself a divorcee who might already have children but be too old to conceive, thereby limiting the chances of having a family of your own. While being a stepfather can be rewarding, neither of these choices is ideal for a man entering the second half of his life, unless of course you are adamant about not wanting your own kids or if you relish the challenge of a much younger partner. Alternatively, you could weigh up the pros and cons and decide to make a commitment in your late twenties or early thirties, which seems to be the optimum time to settle down and start a family.

This level of pragmatism will involve a little forward thinking on your part. Are you willing to let go of your lothario fantasies and commit to a long-term relationship while you are still in your prime? Of course, there will be plenty of imponderables and sacrifices to consider along the way. There is no guarantee, for instance, that you will meet your life partner in that short window of opportunity between the ages of twenty-seven and thirty-four, although it's probably no coincidence that most couples end up marrying at around this age, suggesting that biological considerations force us into making a decision. But what if you choose to ignore conventional wisdom by refusing to compromise? How long will you keep searching for your 'ideal' partner? Maybe you will just continue waiting and hope that perfection falls into your lap before old age ruins your chances.

If you happen to be reading this in your twenties, how do you see your future? You may still be excited by the idea of playing the field – and, yes, there is plenty of short-term fun to be had if you are one of the tiny minority of men who attract lots of female attention. But consider your future.

By forcing us to behave responsibly, the institution of marriage grounds us, giving us a purpose beyond personal gratification. A willingness to abandon fecklessness and adopt responsibility is key for anyone hoping to live a more meaningful life. What we lose in self-actualisation we gain in emotional security and the satisfaction of putting another person's needs before our own. Then there is the sheer cosiness of sharing your life with a fellow traveller. So much of what we require for a meaningful life is embodied within marriage, even though at times you may want to kill each other. So, forget about fireworks and finding 'the one'; choose someone you can rub along with, someone who 'gets' you. Rein in your expectations and you should be fine. Oh, and try not to leave it too late.

Having found someone who ticks enough of the right boxes (don't be greedy) you'll need to discover their 'love language'. In his 1992 bestseller *The 5 Love Languages*, author Gary Chapman outlines the five most common ways we express and receive love:

Receiving gifts

Quality time

Words of affirmation

Acts of service

Physical touch

Chapman reveals that most of us tend to give love in the way we'd like to receive it. So, if your partner's love language is 'acts of service', for instance, she may be confused and disappointed when you do the washing–up but don't see cleaning dishes as anything other than a household chore. That might be because your love language is 'words of affirmation'. Although expressing her feelings for you verbally might not come naturally, she will need to become fluent in your love language so that you can both express the sort of intimacy needed to sustain a relationship. Expressing love for someone in a language they understand is a sure sign of maturity and shows you are ready to take the relationship to the next stage.[18]

A note on marriage

Those who undermine the institution of marriage by dismissing it as 'just a piece of paper' are fundamentally missing the point. By committing to a lifelong partner, we acknowledge the profound link between connection and meaning. In Act Two, we like to keep our options open, casting around for connection while shying away from commitment. Through trial and error, we come to realise the hollowness of shallow encounters. In Act Three, marriage's solemn vows offer us a clear path out of the loneliness of self-interest. Instead of rushing around chasing fickle fantasies, we start to accept limitations and embrace gentle humility and a simple, dignified life.

In our dogged pursuit of individual autonomy, we have succeeded in maligning the very institutions designed to foster long-lasting fulfilment. We need to reject the shallow promise of self-interest and accept that meaningful connection thrives within certain parameters. Committing to a set of principles designed to offer stability means we must embrace sacrifice. Failure to live up to those principles must therefore come with consequences. Marriage loses its meaning if divorce is made too easy. There may be short-term gains to quickie separations, but the foundations of marriage are weakened if the bar for failure is set too low. Marriage only works if the stakes are high, which is why the 'it's only a piece of paper' argument misses the point. Contained within the tenets of that humble document are profound truths about what it means to live a meaningful life. By signing up to these powerful proclamations, you pledge to turn your back on shallow connections and imbue your relationship with seriousness and meaning.

The standard wedding vows can be traced back to *The Book of Common Prayer* by Thomas Cranmer, Archbishop of Canterbury. They were first published in 1549 and are as wise today as they were back then. Let's take a closer look at what these ancient vows teach us about what it means to live a meaningful life:

'To have and to hold' connection comes when I accept another person into my life

'From this day forward' committing to lasting connection unleashes meaning

'For better for worse' but meaning comes with sacrifice

'For richer for poorer' the sacrifice of putting other people's needs before my own

'In sickness and in health' the sacrifice of not running away from the sort of responsibility that gives life meaning

'To love and to cherish' through selfless devotion to others I make the world a better place

'Till death us do part' committing to a life-long connection makes for a meaningful life

So now you are married

Well done, you made the right decision. Now the real work begins. The first thing you need to know about marriage is that you have to commit 100 per cent, no half measures, no hedging bets, no 'seeing how it goes' and definitely no FOMO (fear of missing out). You are in this for the long haul, and that is something to celebrate. Possibly for the first time in your life you have made a written assurance to place another person's needs beyond your own. This is the very definition of mature love.

The next thing you need to know about marriage is that the honeymoon period is short-lived – usually between six months and a year. This sobering truth can often come as a nasty surprise to bickering couples who only six months earlier were expressing undying love for one another in front of a priest. But a healthy marriage needs more than a flying start if it is to survive. Just because you've chosen a path to meaning does not preclude you from suffering. Indeed, with so much at stake, a meaningful life can actually make suffering seem more intense. But that is the price we must pay for delving deeper.

During that first year of marriage, your relationship will seem new and exciting; you may still be learning things about each other and enjoying first experiences together. Married life only really begins when you come back down to earth. Once the novelty of that magical first year has worn off, one of the biggest challenges you will face is how to cope with conflict.

Arguments are of course a normal part of any relationship, but they need to be managed so that disagreements don't turn into resentments. Before making the leap, make sure you are both in agreement on key issues such as schooling for the kids, where you want to be long term (city or countryside?) and the best way to manage your finances. This will help mitigate tensions further down the line. Many churches now include compulsory marriage-preparation classes that can help make sense of your new life together.

Disagreements usually arise when two people with different ways of looking at the world try to understand each other. Unresolved childhood traumas and your own strange idiosyn-crasies will only add to the friction, so talk to trusted friends or have regular couple's therapy if it helps.

Knowing how to stay connected even when you feel a million miles apart is a vital skill you will need to cultivate early on in your marriage. Talking through problems as they occur will prevent a build-up of resentment, passive aggressiveness and self-righteous indignation. Don't wait – tell your wife when you feel upset or angry. Listen to Brené Brown's TED Talk on the importance of vulnerability within relationships, and don't be afraid to express how you feel.[19] Try not to tiptoe around difficult issues – telling it like it is but with kindness should help get to the nub of the problem before things turn nasty.

If you and your partner find yourselves bickering about who cleans the bath, you may need to look a little deeper to find out what's really going on. We often hide our frustrations in trivial rows because facing up to reality can seem too over-whelming. But you need to find out what's really irking you both. Has one of you gone off sex? Have you stopped listening to each other? Is work getting you down? Are you feeling emasculated about your wife's career success? Has your rela-tionship become stale because you've stopped communicating? These deeper, unresolved issues are probably at the root of your arguments. Fail to engage with them and petty spats will con-tinue to wear you both down. Be brave, always focus on the matter in hand and wherever possible retain a lightness of touch however anxious you might be feeling. Humour can quickly dispel brooding discontentment. Try to laugh at yourself and at the absurdity of your predicaments. Understand that there will always be conflicts in your marriage; your job is to remain calm and to see both sides of the story however much you may think you are right.

A successful marriage depends on your willingness to connect emotionally. When your partner makes a request for connection, or a 'bid' as the marriage counsellor John Gottman puts it, you need to be able to acknowledge and respond to that request with kindness. Gottman found that these brief moments of emotional connection are what bind couples together; dismiss, ignore or fail to respond positively and your relationship will eventually wither and die.[20]

If your wife stops to admire a sunset, for instance, she is not merely commentating on the beauty of the setting sun; she is requesting a response from you, a sign that you are engaged and supportive, that you are willing to connect over the glories of nature, or whatever it might happen to be. Once she has made her bid, you then have a choice: either you can 'turn towards' or 'turn away' from the bid. Your wife's enthusiasm for the sunset might seem trivial or silly, but how you respond will reveal a lot about the state of your relationship. The point is, your wife thinks the sunset worthy of your attention, so whether you like sunsets or not is immaterial; you need to be willing to celebrate in her joy. Remember, our appreciation of something moving or beautiful takes on greater significance when the person we love shares in our enthusiasm. An unwillingness to engage in your partner's bids means you are not fully committed to the relationship.

The Gottman Institute studied more than 3,000 couples and found that these bidding interactions had a profound effect on marital well-being. Couples who had divorced after a six-year follow-up had 'turned towards bids' 33 per cent of the time. In other words, only three in ten of their bids for emotional connection had been met with intimacy. Couples who had remained together after six years had 'turned towards bids' 87 per cent of the time. Gottman is able to predict with up to 94 per cent certainty whether couples will have broken up or stayed together years after their initial decision to get married.[21]

Next time you are focusing on work and your wife decides to come over and stroke your hair, don't pull away or tell her you are too busy to respond. Instead, stop what you are doing and show how much you appreciate her gesture by offering to stroke her hair too, or you could kiss her cheek and tell her how much you love her. Meeting a bid only takes a moment. You need to decide what is more important: finishing a spreadsheet or engaging with your wife. It may sound cheesy, but you'd be amazed how neglectful we become of these tender moments, especially during and after conflicts when they are needed the most.

The Gottman Institute study concludes that there are 'disasters' and 'masters' of relationships. The 'disasters' tend to resort to negative tropes such as defensiveness, contempt, criticism and stonewalling, while the 'masters' display more positive traits, such as curiosity, admiration, affection and a willingness to adapt. Rather than always needing to be right, masters are much better listeners during arguments. They lean in even when they feel like leaning out.

The research also found that conflicts are often triggered when heartbeats rise above a certain rate, so it's vital to recognise when stress levels are building – if there's a pounding in your chest and your head feels as though it's about to explode, you'll know it is time to walk away from the conflict. Go to another room, yell into a cushion or just take some long, deep breaths. Remember that most arguments erupt when we fail to connect. During disagreements, always give your wife the benefit of the doubt and try not to take everything she says to heart.

Show warmth and affection even when you feel like running away, and don't punish her with moodiness, sulking or passive aggression. Tenderness can heal painful wounds and help bring equilibrium and perspective back to your relationship. We all crave warmth, especially when we feel vulnerable, so give icy disdain the cold shoulder.

In the end, it won't be raging arguments, financial disasters or disputes about household chores that decide the fate of your marriage; it will be your willingness to engage in those fleeting moments of connection, those precious little jewels of acknowledgement that show you are there and that you care.

Claustrophobia

Marriage keeps us grounded but can also feel suffocating at times. The poet W. B. Yeats advised lovers to 'never give all the heart'.[22] Retaining a level of independence while remaining committed and passionate keeps us resilient and stops us from becoming codependent. Knowing that you are capable of looking after yourself will ease your partner's burden of responsibility. And if your world suddenly comes crashing down, you will have a reservoir of strength to draw upon.

It may be a cliché, but you really do need to give each other space. Intimacy is vital for a healthy relationship, but so too is a good night's sleep. Sharing a marital home can be intense, so sleeping in separate bedrooms might help ease the pressure. After all, one of you is bound to be either a snorer or a tosser-and-turner. Lack of sleep can make us irritable and argumentative, so do everything in your power to mitigate unnecessary tension.

We don't all have the luxury of separate bathrooms, but they are a good idea wherever possible. It's easy to see why couples fall out over bathroom arrangements. Men spend hours on the loo; women spend hours in the bath. Men leave stubble all over the sink and never put the loo seat down. Women need space for make-up bags and complain when the loo seat is left up. Relationships are all about conflict limitation, so make sure you give each other room to breathe.

Similarly, if you are both self-employed and work from home, rent an outside office if you can; leave the house every morning as if you were going to work and only return home at the end of the working day. As well as giving you structure and routine, having a separate workspace might just save your relationship. Spending time apart doesn't mean you love each other any less, but it does keep things fresh by allowing you to miss one another, a key component of any successful relationship.

A note from social reformer Henry Ward Beecher

'Hold yourself responsible for a higher standard than anybody else expects of you. Never excuse yourself. Never pity yourself. Be a hard master to yourself and be lenient to everybody else.'[23]

Division of labour

Equality within a relationship means you can adapt far more easily to changing circumstances. Arguments about who does what around the house can be defused by adopting a more pragmatic approach to mundane tasks. Try to think of house-work less as a chore and more of a courtesy to the person you love and with whom you share a home. Resentments build when one or other of you isn't pulling their weight. Sit down with your partner early on in the relationship and make a list of all the household chores you despise most. Then decide who does what. If you can't stand ironing, for instance, agree to vacuum the floors instead. Together you will come up with an equitable way to apportion responsibility, meaning you will never have to argue about who empties the dishwasher again.

Negotiate and cooperate with your partner; don't expect to be one thing and don't expect her to be one thing either. Make a plan that suits you both and stick to it. Remember, relationships aren't about a struggle for power or dominance. A good marriage thrives on cooperation not competition. You can't be all things to all people, but you can find a healthy balance. So, be strong and dependable when you need to be, but don't be afraid to open up emotionally. A confident, well-adjusted man should be able to do both.

Carl Jung believed that humans were a complex mix of feminine and masculine qualities and that life was a struggle to balance these two competing forces. He argued that men had to embrace masculinity before they could embrace their anima (the female inside the male).[24] Once you become aware of the split, find a way to balance your masculine and feminine sides. For example, rein in aggressive argumentativeness (too much masculine) and avoid getting caught up in futile emotions (too much feminine). Draw on both sides of your gendered self and become a fully functioning man.

Your libido

Waning libidos are a common cause of friction within marriages. Our ability or willingness to have sex is dependent on many different factors, some of which are beyond our control. Low self-esteem, for example, can have a devastating impact on your ability to perform. If you feel stressed at work or depressed at home, sexual desire will be one of the first things to go. Over time, one or other of you may lose interest in sex altogether; this isn't uncommon but can lead to deep resentments and blame. Adjusting to your partner's changing sexual appetite takes patience and understanding. That initial intensity you both felt during the honeymoon period will most likely fall away at some point. Even so, it's hard not to take the rejection personally; sex, after all, is supposed to be a physical manifestation of the love you feel for each other. But it's important to remember that the libido is a notoriously fickle beast, seemingly with a mind of its own. Sex drives can vanish overnight, so you need to eschew embarrassment and be willing to talk openly about the possible causes. In middle age, libidos naturally start to subside, so reassure your partner that your lack of interest is not to do with her. It may be that the drudgery of everyday life is sapping you of energy, or perhaps you are worrying about money or the future. These are perfectly legitimate reasons, but you need to be honest. If it's the case that you no longer find your wife physically attractive, then she needs to know. It's possible that you still love her but feel ambivalent towards her sexually. This is no one's fault, of course, but it's vital that you keep the lines of communication open to avoid hurt feelings. Don't make excuses such as blaming tiredness or work pressures. You might just need some couple's counselling to help bring any deep-seated problems to the surface. Your lack of libido may well be temporary. Sex drives can return as quickly as they disappeared, so try not to despair. Do everything you can to keep your marriage alive during these tricky emotional storms. Even if you have fallen out of love with your partner, there's still hope. Over the course of a marriage, love ebbs and flows too.

A note on what to do if your sex life has become stale and uninspiring

You may be feeling despondent about the quality of your sex life, but it might just need a kick-start. After you have been together for a while, it's easy to take each other for granted. This is when you need to start working on your relationship if you want to keep the flame alive. Making an effort shows you still care. Treat yourselves to a night out at least once a week. Surprise your wife with a romantic dinner on a boring Tuesday night when you'd normally be home watching Netflix, or arrange a weekend spa retreat. Take it in turns to organise weekends away and rekindle those sparks of passion and energy that brought you together in the first place.

Here are some other suggestions to keep you both interested:

Unexpected treats If you see something you think your wife might like, don't wait until her birthday. Wrap it up and leave it on her pillow today.

Be spontaneous When you live together, life can become overly predictable, so every now and then shake yourself out of complacency by doing something impetuous. Maybe you fancy a trip to Amsterdam or a beach break. Don't think about it; just do it. We often enjoy ourselves far more when we free ourselves from the burden of expectation and act spontaneously.

Take time out to miss each other Go and stay with friends for the weekend or rent a cottage on your own. You need time apart in order to appreciate time together. Variety will stop your relationship going sour.

The importance of male friendships

Seventeenth-century romanticism, from which we derive the idea of romantic love, believed that a spouse should provide us with all our emotional needs, from unlimited sex to deep platonic friendship. But no one person can or should be the bearer of all that is good in our lives. When problems arise, we need the steady hand of outside companionship to guide us through. Take comfort in close male friendships during times of existential doubt. These deep, dependable links to your past know you better than anyone and will always be there for you. When you feel the weight of the world pressing down, why not call up a friend and arrange to go for a long hike together. Think of it as walking therapy. Open up and share any pent-up fears you might have, then encourage your friend to do likewise. Having a dependable companion by your side as you marvel at nature will help put any problems into perspective. Anxieties will lessen once they have been aired. Marriage is a delicate balance of sharing and sparing, so try not to burden your wife with too many existential worries. Save them for your friends; that's what they are for.

A note on powerlessness and vulnerability

The power dynamic between men and women is changing so rapidly many of us are struggling to keep up. Adding to our confusion is a sense that not all women are choosing to transition into independent I-don't-know-how-she-does-it go-getters. Many less-driven women remain wedded to the old-fashioned ideal of staying home to look after the kids without the need for extra validation in the form of a high-powered job. With women's expectations in a state of flux, we are having to interpret all kinds of mixed messages. Some of you may be struggling to keep up with your partners' ever-changing demands; expecting you to be strong and decisive one minute, sensitive and nurturing the next. It's important to open up and admit when you are struggling. Your wife will understand.

Parenthood

Deciding to become a father is the most important decision you will ever make, so you may be wondering why there is so little in the way of information out there to help guide you through the process. In no other important area of life is responsibility for one's actions taken so lightly. Our attitude to fatherhood is positively cavalier when compared with, say, the adoption of a pet. Enquire about adopting a dog from a rescue centre, for instance, and the first thing they make you aware of is the enormous responsibility that comes with pet ownership, from the relentless exercise routines to exorbitant vet bills. If you are still determined to go ahead, you will have to prove that you are a responsible homeowner with a garden big enough to accommodate an energetic, attention-seeking hound. There will be forms to fill in, fees to pay and agreements to sign. An official might pay you a home visit to check on your living standards.

Remarkably, no such checks exist for those wanting to raise a child; no government leaflets, no costing analysis, no examinations or assessments required, and no officials will come knocking on your door. Indeed, your only real consideration will be whether you feel 'ready'.

Perhaps it would be more responsible if we were all compelled to sign a marriage-style contract before giving birth, vowing to love and cherish our newborn until death us do part. Certainly, you should ask yourself why you want to have children. Is it a casual whim? Do you feel under pressure from a spouse or family member? Are you worried that you might be running out of time? Perhaps you think a baby will heal a rift in your marriage. Or is wanting a child purely an expression of the love you feel for your wife? Whatever your reasons for wanting a child, you'll need to consider all the implications before making your decision.

Childrearing – the facts

- **How much?** The cost of raising a child will depend on your personal circumstances, and no two families are alike. The most recent report from Child Poverty Action Group reveals that the basic cost of raising a child until the age of eighteen is £75,436 for a couple and £102,627 for a lone-parent family. If you include childcare, these costs rise dramatically to £155,100 and £187,100. That's more than £8,000 per annum for a couple and more than £10,000 for a lone-parent family. (The average cost of childcare in the UK is between £220 and £250 a week per child under two years old.) Nappies alone cost around £260 per annum. On an average annual income of £29,000, a lone-parent family would need to set aside a third of their income.[25] If you decide to send your child to private school, you'll need to add another £17,000 on average per annum to the mix. As you can see, this doesn't leave much for basic living costs, let alone mortgages, holidays and home appliances. Make sure you budget meticulously.

- **How will it change my life?** Remove any lingering expectations and remember you are learning something from scratch. Raising a child up to the age of eighteen is hard but meaningful work. You will need patience and nerves of steel. The weight of responsibility will seem almost unbearable at times. Sleep deprivation and boredom will put an enormous strain on your marriage. You will no longer be the centre of attention and may feel rejected by your wife. Tempers will flare. Don't be afraid to hire professional help if you can afford it and be grateful for hand-me-downs from family and friends.

- **Disruption to your daily routine** You will be learning on the job, so expect to make plenty of mistakes. Adjusting to parenthood is a process of trial and error. There will be good days and bad days, so don't beat yourself up when you get things wrong.

- **Keep it simple** Your baby doesn't need as much as you think. Forget about all those fluffy toys and expensive gadgets. As long as they are healthy and happy, fed and watered, then you are doing a good job.

- **It's no longer about you** Becoming a father is one of the most meaningful things you can do in your life, but you must be prepared to let go of your ego.

Fatherhood is not a decision you should take lightly. Consider the practicalities and try not to be swayed by family pressures or the misguided belief that a child will somehow save your failing marriage. Sit down with your wife and have an honest conversation about the many complications and practicalities of parenthood. Consider your circumstances carefully and then ask the following questions:

- How will we deal with the stress and lack of sleep?

- How will parenthood change our lives, and what sacrifices will we have to make?

- Can we afford to have children right now? Let's break down the costs.

- Do we have enough space?

- Is our relationship strong enough to weather the storm of those difficult first years?

- How are we going to apportion responsibility, and will we need outside help?

- Can we afford a nanny?

- Are we both going to need to work?

- Are you prepared to be a stay-at-home dad if necessary?

- Are you mentally and physically up to the challenge?

A note on how not to feel lonely in a marriage

If you've recently had children, your wife's focus will have understandably shifted, so it might come as a shock not to be the centre of her universe any more. Don't take her lack of attention personally and give her the space she needs. Be supportive and kind, and do your fair share of nappy changing. If you're feeling ignored or left out, talk to other dads. Every relationship takes effort and a certain amount of sacrifice, but marriage in particular can be full of unexpected challenges that only intensify once children come on the scene.

Think long and hard about the implications of having children and talk through every detail with your partner, because once your children are born time will no longer be your own. Going out will become a logistical and expensive nightmare, so don't be one of those couples who look back with regret at all the opportunities you missed when you were child free. Make the most of your freedom while you still have it. Speak to friends with kids and find out what sort of life changes they had to make. Don't be afraid to ask for advice and aim to have children by your mid thirties, because the next act of your life will have a whole new set of problems to deal with.

Enjoy your freedom before committing to children

Here is a list of all those things you will regret if you don't do them now:

1. Visit as many of the great art galleries as you can.

2. Go to the theatre and cinema as much as you can.

3. Treat yourself to a meal in a restaurant at least once a week if you can afford it.

4. Head to Europe and enjoy romantic city breaks with your wife.

5. Immerse yourself in different cultures and ways of life while you still have the chance.

6. Go for regular hikes in the countryside and spend as much time as you can with good friends. Once you have kids, time will no longer be your own.

Relationships and parenthood – in summary

- We are all flawed and ridiculous in our own ways – don't imagine you are any different
- Marriages fall apart when we fail to acknowledge our partners' bids for connection
- Try to put arguments behind you, and don't bear grudges
- Maintain a lightness of touch in all things
- Embrace your silly, playful side, and don't take yourself seriously
- Be tender and warm even when you feel cold

- Try not to take everything to heart, and give your partner the benefit of the doubt. Don't point the finger of blame

- Relationships can be intense, so give each other space. Spending time apart allows you to miss each other

- Adjust to your partner's changing sexual appetite

- Respect and value the ancient institution of marriage, and remember it is so much more than 'just a piece of paper'

- Don't allow anger and resentments to fester. Be open and honest with each other about how you really feel and avoid blame

- Retain separate bathrooms wherever possible

- Share household chores. Remember relationships are about cooperation not competition

- Set clear boundaries, and let your partner know when they have crossed a line

- Think hard about whether you are ready and can afford to have children

- Be strong and dependable when you need to be, but don't be afraid to open up emotionally

Act Four
Work and Providing

Jealous in honour, sudden and quick in quarrel,
seeking the bubble reputation

The way we work may be changing, but the 'primary provider' instinct remains hardwired into many men's DNA. Traditionally, men were expected to be the main breadwinners, leaving women to look after the home and family. But since the decline in manufacturing and the rise of digital and AI technology, most workplaces now favour brains over brawn. In a few short decades, the jobs market has changed beyond recognition, leading to a profound shift in men's and women's expectations of each other. This dramatic turnaround has bled into the domestic sphere too, with men now expected to up their game when it comes to childcare and domestic chores. But for many of us, work still defines who we are.

While having a worthwhile job certainly adds purpose to your life, you should strive to be more than what you do for a living. So much male anxiety comes from our need to compete in the jobs market, and the tendency is always to compare up, meaning however successful we become there will always be someone a few rungs further up the ladder. The inclination to downplay our own achievements and exaggerate the achievements of others can drive us mad with envy to the point where we start to resent our friends' successes.

But what do we actually mean by a 'successful' career? Is it just about the accumulation of wealth and self-esteem, or should we define success by more meaningful criteria, such as how much others appreciate us for the good we do?

If you are trapped in a meaningless, dead-end job, think about how you might free yourself. Just because you've been doing the same soul-destroying work for thirty years doesn't mean you have to continue destroying your soul for another thirty. Maybe you have chosen to stay in your rut because leaving seems too daunting. Or maybe you have family who rely on you for support. Of course, you should act responsibly by putting the needs of your family first, but be aware that age can make us increasingly risk-averse. Rather than putting up with a lifetime of drudgery, consider whether there might be other, more meaningful jobs that might suit you better and that don't require years of retraining.

If changing careers is out of the question, think laterally and take bold steps to make your current job more interesting. We spend around 90,000 hours,[1] or a third of our life, at work, so see if there's a way to shake things up a bit, because if your job makes you miserable, chances are you will take that misery home with you. Don't let the pressures of work impinge on your family life. Slow down if your job is causing you anxiety and try to leave work stresses where they belong — at work. Consider what you might lose by turning your work life around, other than the security of remaining unfulfilled. Then think about all the possible gains. And don't forget to make provision for your old age. Talk to a financial adviser, calculate how much you are going to need and take out an appropriate pension plan.

Busyness Olympics

Anxieties about work can become particularly acute in early middle age when many of us are still scrabbling around trying to make our mark, worrying about whether we are achieving enough. We look at friends and assume they are all happier and more fulfilled than we could ever be. Most of us work such long hours that when we do finally slow down, we don't know what to do with ourselves. This need to remain active at all times has led to a sort of busyness–derangement syndrome, in which we end up judging our worth by how exhausted we feel at the end of the day. Sensing that friends and colleagues are busier than we are can send us into a spiral of inadequacy. Many of us latch onto the busyness bug so we don't have to think about deeper, more pressing concerns, such as why we are here and what we are for. Focusing all our energy on pointless purpose might make us feel important, but it certainly doesn't make for a meaningful life. Free yourself from the busyness contagion by taking some time out of your day to gaze off into the middle distance where some of our most profound thoughts are hiding.

Taking time off work

Don't miss out on your offspring's childhood. Prioritise family time together, especially during those precious early years. If you have a daughter, show her by your conduct how a decent, responsible man should act. As her primary male role model, your behaviour will determine how she sees other men; future boyfriends will need to live up to your standards, so make sure those standards are high. You are her male template; how you behave now will stay with her for life. If you choose to neglect your fatherly duties because you are too wrapped up in work, she will start to lose faith in you and in men more generally. So, make time for your daughter. Show an interest in the things she loves, help her with her homework, and when the time is right warn her about the dangers of unwanted pregnancies, while stressing the importance of stable, loving relationships.

Retreats

With so much pressure to provide for our families, it's good to know that there are places we can go to talk through problems with like-minded individuals. As work and relationship patterns shift, many of us are now actively seeking answers to some of life's big, existential questions concerning who we are and what we are for. An entire industry has grown up around what many are calling a 'crisis of masculinity', with international organisations, men's groups, weekend retreats and online discussion forums catering to a growing army of disaffected males.

The ManKind Project's 'Experimental Personal Development Programmes', for instance, offer global support networks where men gather in male-only retreats to discuss anxieties, share problems, reflect on past traumas and misdemeanours, and reconnect with 'positive masculine energies'. The MKP's 'New Warrior Training Adventure' offers a modern take on the old 'hero's journey', with rural retreats across the globe offering wounded men the chance to rebuild shattered confidences while rejecting vicarious lives lived through 'movies, television, addiction and distraction' in favour of meaningful connection. Participants are encouraged to find their own adventures 'in real time and surrounded by other men'. The emphasis is on improving men's relationships through greater self-knowledge, self-reflection and self-growth. Participants are encouraged to show up as the 'man, husband, partner, father and brother' they were 'born to be'. Too many of us have grown up without a clear masculine template, so we fail to take responsibility for bad parenting, problems at work and dysfunctional relationships. Team-building exercises are an important part of the man–camp experience, reminding men about the value of cooperation and personal responsibility. There is an emphasis on competitive games because you can tell a lot about a man by the way he behaves on the sports field. There are the generous team–player types, for example, who selflessly sacrifice personal glory for the greater good of the game, and the egotistical maniacs who don't care what happens as long as they score the winning goal.

Many of the men attending workshops struggle to cope with mind-numbing jobs, while others worry about unemployment and how they are going to provide for their families. Some feel emasculated by a changing jobs market that seems to favour female talents. Over recent years, a pattern of behaviour has emerged where men seem willing to play along with traditional gender-role expectations early on in relationships – competent, successful man impresses potential long-term partner with an abundance of candlelit dinners, sparkling repartee and great sex. But when the frightened, insecure man-child hiding beneath the facade finally emerges, the power dynamic shifts dramatically, resulting in disappointment for her, a loss of confidence from him and eventual break-up for both.

As men we need to hold on to our dignity and be proud of who we are even when work and relationship difficulties over-whelm us. It's natural to feel anxious when faced with all that pressure to succeed, but while we mustn't be ashamed to express our vulnerability, we should also hold on to traditional masculine coping strategies such as stoicism and fortitude. Many of us have learnt through experience to keep our emo-tions in check, not because we are emotionally illiterate but because a certain amount of restraint helps keep us resilient when times are tough. We all have our own reasons for remain-ing stoical, and for the most part that stoicism serves us well; trying times often call for quiet, selfless determination rather than noisy self-pity. Juggling a stressful work and home life, dealing with tragedy, being there for a friend in need often requires us to keep our own emotions in check. This ability to regulate our feelings according to circumstance can be benefi-cial and is largely pragmatic rather than some kind of pathological patriarchal dysfunctional. Remaining strong can help us deal with work-related problems, a rocky divorce or the death of a loved one. But while it's important not to buckle under pressure, we should avoid burying our emotions too deeply so that we struggle to open up to our authentic selves. Even now, many of us have been taught to believe that express-ing any sort of emotion is self-indulgent or something only women are allowed to do. Whatever life throws at us, we need to find our emotional balance: knowing when to let go and when to hold back. And it's important to remember that nei-ther sex has a monopoly on suffering.

Fortunately, there are now places men can go to talk through work and relationship difficulties with female facilitators whose sole job is to listen and empathise. Retreats run exclusively by women for the benefit of men focus on rebuilding trust between the sexes. For most of the male attendees, love and respect for women has turned to bitterness and resentment. Many are simply confused about women's expectations and are in desperate need of female validation. By sharing their anxieties with empathetic women, men who have lost all hope gain invaluable insights into why they struggle to maintain a healthy work–life balance (too needy, too lazy, too ready to play the blame game, too angry, too demanding, too work-obsessed).

If you are in need of help but don't have time to go on a three-day retreat, there are plenty of local men's groups you can join, either online or at organised events. The ManKind Project, for instance, holds regular support groups all across the country. At first you might struggle to open up in front of a bunch of random men, but once you overcome your shyness you will find the experience both moving and rewarding. What's more, it will come as a great relief to discover you are not the only one struggling.

Unemployment

Because of our traditional primary-provider status, during times of recession and job loss, we are often ill equipped or unwilling to adapt, with many of us seeing domestic duties as secondary to paid work. This imbalance of power needs to shift if men and women are to become truly equal. If you are unemployed, because of redundancy, a lack of qualifications or because you were passed over at work for someone younger, it's natural to feel a sense of shame. Having all that extra time on your hands can seem disorientating, so it's important to add structure to your day. Use the extra time to feed and expand your mind. Read extensively and try not to sit around all day feeling sorry for yourself. Remember life is painfully short, so get out there and start living. Just because you are between jobs doesn't mean you should cut yourself off from friends and family. Being out of work may have dented your pride, but with grit and determination you can get through this. You might want to consider returning to higher education, for example, although you may need to take on some part-time work to tide you over.

If you have a passion in life, now is the perfect time to pursue it; start your own business or talk to influential friends who might be able to help. Depending on the state of the economy, you might be out of work for some time, so instead of sinking into despondency, take advantage of your newfound freedom. Remember, time is our most precious commodity, so use it wisely. Don't let unemployment make you lazy; take the opportunity to do all the things you never had time to do when you were preoccupied with work. Explore your neighbourhood and wander the historic streets and alleyways. If you're short of cash, spending quality time with friends doesn't cost you a penny and is one of the most meaningful things you can do with your time. Most major museums in the UK are free to visitors, so take advantage of some of the world's greatest art collections right here on your doorstep. However frightened you feel about the future, remember that humans are incredibly adaptable and resourceful. Learn to live with less and concentrate on the life of the mind while you have the chance.

A note on homelessness

For the most vulnerable in society, unemployment can have devastating consequences. On a freezing night in December 2018, Gyula Remes, a forty-three-year-old homeless man, died in a grim underpass outside the Houses of Parliament in central London. Another homeless person who had been sleeping nearby told reporters, 'He was blue last night, and everyone was just walking past him like he didn't matter.'[2] The average age of a homeless man at death is forty-four, half the average male lifespan. According to the charity Homeless Link, of the 4,751 individuals counted or estimated to be sleeping rough in England in 2017, 3,965 were male, 653 female and 133 gender unknown.[3]

Lewis's story is typical of many homeless young men. Kicked out of his family home due to crime and a drug-related lifestyle, he found himself in desperate straits. Unable to find work, he drifted through the cracks and at twenty-nine ended up on the streets of Birmingham begging for food and relying on handouts from outreach workers. 'I just messed up,' he said, but messing up as a vulnerable man can come with a heavy price. The lack of a father figure in many instances combined with a lack of direction and a sense of hopelessness and isolation means young men like Lewis are simply unprepared for the vagaries of adult life: 'I just need money. I need a nine to five. I need hope.' According to Homeless Link, homeless men are more likely to use drugs, smoke and have an alcohol problem than homeless women: 77 per cent of the 1,248 homeless people surveyed who used drugs and alcohol to cope with mental-health issues were men; 72 per cent of the 426 homeless people surveyed who didn't receive support for mental-health problems, but said it would help them, were men. In short, homeless men's mental and physical needs simply aren't being met. We all need to do what we can to help. Volunteer at a homeless charity, give regular donations to Shelter and next time you see someone living rough don't cross the street or walk the other way. Ask if they need help. Buy them food, drink and a warm blanket. Find out where the nearest homeless shelter is and offer to take them there. Love your neighbour as yourself and treat them the way you would like to be treated. Next time it might be you living rough.

When you feel you can't go on

Before ending his life in a dingy Australian hotel room on 23 June 1968, comedian Tony Hancock wrote a bleak suicide note that read: 'Things seemed to go wrong too many times.' Aged just forty-four, Hancock appeared to have it all, but inside he was a mess, racked by the sort of melancholy and frustration common amongst many of our greatest funny men. Even at the height of his fame he became fascinated by suicide, although he often expressed a distaste for the fatalism of others. The comedian Charlie Drake remembers a conversation during which Hancock suggested they make a suicide pact.

Unlike many men suffering from mental torment, Hancock never shied away from his demons; in a moving 1960 interview with John Freeman he talked about the nature of comedy and how human affectation could be both comic and sad. By pricking pomposity and exposing pretence, Hancock claimed to reveal deep truths about the tragedy of human existence. He admits in the interview that he never expected to be happy, believing happiness to be little more than an illusion.[4] Here we see a man at the height of his powers exposed, a lonely, isolated man willing to admit that fame and wealth had brought him little in the way of comfort, a man with three sports cars who couldn't even drive, a childless, middle-aged man haunted by his father's early death, focusing all his energy on work to avoid having to face reality. In the last few days of his life, mired in alcoholism and teetering on the edge of self-destruction, Hancock consulted a medium who fed him trite messages from beyond the grave – the final straw perhaps for a man whose life had lost all meaning.

Hancock's is an all too familiar story of a man driven to the edge by crippling self-doubt and high levels of anxiety. Perhaps you are going through a similarly turbulent time in your life, when nothing seems to make sense and everything you hoped would bring satisfaction has instead left you wanting.

In the same year that 597 homeless people died on the streets of the UK (84 per cent of whom were men), 4,382 adult males ended their life voluntarily, an average of twelve men per day. With suicide now the biggest killer of men under forty-five, the reason for this unprecedented rise has been the cause of much debate.[5] For anti–patriarchal activists, men are turning their misery and aggression on themselves because 'traditional' masculinity has robbed them of their emotional literacy. Organisations such as the APA appear to be saying that if only men had the courage to abandon these unhealthy gender tropes and embrace vulnerability, then maybe they'd find the strength to carry on. Ironically, it is traditional masculine traits such as resilience and courage that have helped us during times of crisis. Perhaps these are the kinds of qualities suicidal men should be drawing upon. It is probably no coincidence that the activists calling for men to abandon traditional masculine coping strategies are the very same ideologues seeking an end to 'the patriarchy'. Then again, some of us have become so hung up on the idea that we need to remain strong at any cost that we fail to seek help when we really need it. Perhaps the spike in male suicide is down to more prosaic factors such as unemployment, debt, mental health, incarceration, addiction, family breakdown, fatherlessness and enforced separation from children through the family-court system. It's important to understand that asking for help is never a sign of weakness.

Telling men they are a danger to themselves and to others might also have some bearing on whether they consider life worth living or not. Sadness, anger, disappointment, feelings of betrayal, isolation, loneliness, fear, confusion – these are all natural human responses to the problems life throws at us, so don't feel guilty if they creep up on you occasionally or even frequently. If, however, those same emotions leave you feeling overwhelmed or unable to function in your daily life, if you struggle to get out of bed in the morning or are contemplating ending it all, then you need to seek urgent help. Don't hesitate or worry about what others might think. Talk to your friends and family. If they aren't forthcoming, there are professionals out there who can help. Therapy is no longer the preserve of super-rich celebrities. Check the British Association for Counselling and Psychotherapy website for a list of qualified therapists in your area – some work on a sliding scale and only ask you to pay what you can afford.

We all need to keep our mental and emotional health in check. Airing your problems with a professional will help defuse anxiety and keep you on an even keel. During sessions, you might want to explore past traumas and discover how events in your childhood affect your current state of mind and attitude to life. Once you understand how your mind works, you'll be able to put problems into some kind of perspective. If you still feel you can't go on, pick up the phone and ring the Samaritans – it's free and your call will be confidential. Trained facilitators will listen patiently and offer advice where they can. The charity is open twenty-four hours a day, 365 days a year; you can even visit your local branch for a face-to-face chat if you prefer. Although some stigmas persist, issues around mental health are no longer seen as shameful, so if you feel desperate or need advice there's always someone you can turn to. Whatever you do, don't suffer in silence.

Work and providing – in summary

- Seek out meaningful work that you enjoy
- Remember you are more than what you do for a living
- Don't become envious of your friends' career successes
- Learn to adjust to changing circumstances
- Try not to get caught up in the 'Busyness Olympics' – life is not a race
- Join a men's group or attend a weekend retreat and share your problems with like-minded individuals
- Don't miss out on your offspring's childhood by becoming too bogged down in work. If you have a daughter, take an interest in the things she loves. Prioritise family time together, especially during those precious early years
- Don't let unemployment make you lazy
- Enjoy a modest life, and learn to live with less
- If you feel you can't go on, seek help from friends and family, arrange to have some therapy sessions or ring the Samaritans on 116 123 free of charge

Act Five
Middle Age

Full of wise saws and modern instances

The middle years can be a traumatic time as we take stock of our lives. You may start to question all your old assumptions and wonder why nothing seems to make sense any more. Everything appears to be out of kilter. Perhaps you feel a sense of anti-climax; weren't you supposed to have gained wisdom and understanding by now? Instead you feel more confused than ever as you look back with regret at 'the vast shipwreck of your life's esteems' to quote John Clare from his masterful poem 'I Am'.[1] Life hasn't turned out the way you planned, but you can't even remember what the plan was supposed to be. Events just sort of happened, and now here you are, slap bang in the middle of your life, wondering what on earth you are supposed to do next. All you really want is to be given a second chance. Craving the giddy excitement of youth is understandable at this age, but you must try to resist the urge to wallow in nostalgia or seek solace in fleeting, adolescent pleasures. Deal with things as they are, not as you wished they might have been.

The midlife crisis usually hits us between the age of thirty-five and fifty. Typically, we are struck by an overwhelming sense of alienation and disconnect. Life continues around us, and yet we feel strangely locked out, as though staring 'through a glass darkly'. Mind and body may no longer feel connected. Emotionally, we are all over the place, furiously railing against the injustices of the world one minute, sobbing uncontrollably about who knows what the next. We may become irascible, impatient, unpredictable and distant around people we love. The terrible fear that at any moment some awful, debilitating disease might strike us down stalks every ache and pain, of which there are an increasing number. And if we do get carried off before our time, we assume no one will care or even notice that we are gone. At 4 a.m., we lie awake trying to imagine the manner of our passing: will it be swift and painless or years of nursing-home indignity?

Terrified of what the future might hold, we catastrophise and turn inward, losing our lust for life. Some seek comfort in overeating or try to blank out the pain with alcohol. Others may decide the only way out is to do something mad and impetuous. A sudden irrational optimism takes hold; we think we are invincible and can take on the world. Throwing caution to the wind, we make extravagant plans. Some will buy a sports car and head out on the open road, swearing never to return. Others will jack in their boring day job and focus on the magnum opus they have been meaning to write for twenty years. Plenty of us will have affairs with younger women to remind us what it feels like to be alive. Or we hit forty and decide our spouse no longer understands us and the kids are holding us back. Yearning to be free, we move out of the marital home and try to forge a new and better life. No wonder Act Five is littered with so many broken marriages and desperate lives. We start to crave the liberties we think we have lost, forgetting that freedom isn't quite so liberating when school fees and mortgages have to be paid. Once we've dumped our wives, we may decide to ditch our close friends too, in the hope that new ones might be more sympathetic to our plights.

There is something touchingly adolescent about our midlife malaises – the idea that the world no longer understands us, that solace exists anywhere but where we are, the hope that excitement and impulsivity can somehow free us from life's drudgery. Of course, all such attempts to stave off the inevitable will come to nothing. The sports car will only get us so far before it too becomes just another drain on our dwindling resources. Write that epic novel by all means, but don't expect it to be easy, and don't imagine that giving up your day job and moving to a garret will make the agony subside. (Remember the words of Confucius: 'No matter where you go, there you are' – tragically, we can never run away from ourselves.) And don't think that ditching your friends is going to set you free either, even if you feel they may have let you down. Old friends are your anchor to everything that is meaningful. Guard them with your life and never forget how much they mean to you. For many people, forging lasting friendships becomes harder the older we get, so cherish the ones you already have – never take them for granted; they may frustrate and disappoint from time to time, but they are the most important people in your life and a vital link to your past. As for flinging yourself at younger women, your ego may be boosted, you may even feel more alive, but the novelty will soon wear off, and that pretty young fling will end up being just another flawed individual who doesn't really understand you. She will eventually leave you, or you will leave her, by which time your wife will have found out and be filing for divorce.

None of these escape plans will add meaning to your life. Rather than clutching at wretched straws, try to think of middle age as just another tricky transitioning period, a bit like puberty but without the spots. Feeling scared and confused is just something we have to go through in order to reach the next age. The problem is, we have so many negative preconceptions about what middle age is going to be like, based on the people we already know. Some of us will remember what our parents were like and shudder at the thought of gaining a few extra chins and a dubious record collection. Perhaps you have found yourself at a dull house party thinking, 'why am I hanging out with all these old buffers?', only to realise that you are now one of them. You might come across some teenage offspring out in the garden smoking weed and think, I should be having fun with these guys, not stuck inside with a bunch of elderly bores.

It's touching that most of us simply don't feel ready to make the transition into middle age; we might be pushing fifty, but in our heads and hearts we still feel twenty-five. The dreaded midlife crisis is often triggered by profound events – the death of a parent, for instance – and the sudden, horrifying realisation that you are moving inexorably towards the departure lounge. Your deteriorating body and fading looks may also become a source of anguish. You might suddenly lose you hair or your hearing or both. Your eyesight will certainly start to deteriorate, and you will keep losing your glasses, which you will eventually find perched on top of your balding pate. These are just some of the indignities that befall us as we hobble into our forties and fifties. Be prepared for swollen prostate glands and dodgy knees. The crisis itself can creep up on you over a number of years or hit you like a train the moment you turn thirty-five. Either way, you will make it through in the end. And once you emerge on the other side, you will start to realise that ageing isn't quite as terrifying as you feared. In fact, it could just be the making of you.

Don't panic

Wherever you are in your life's journey, the middle years will be a time of deep reflection. You may panic at the sheer speed with which you arrived at this pivotal moment and feel anxious about what lies ahead. Take comfort – there is still plenty of meaning to be had in midlife, and as long as you remain healthy and philosophical, you'll be able to cope with the indignities that may befall you.

The 'andropause'

When you hit middle age, your body starts to change. Joints, muscles and skin all lose their suppleness, and your memory might start to fade. Some of you will even suffer from menopausal-like symptoms. Up until relatively recently it was assumed that men were immune from the 'change of life' endured by middle-aged women. But according to Dr Marion Gluck, a world pioneer in bioidentical hormones, the 'andropause' or 'manopause' should be taken seriously. Although Gluck specialises in helping menopausal women, she has seen a marked increase in the number of men seeking treatment, often at the behest of worried wives and partners: 'Men find it much harder to admit when something is wrong.'[2]

Changing hormone levels in middle age can leave us feeling achy, tired and irritable. Some men complain about a woozy sense of unreality. If you suffer from sudden mood swings or struggle to concentrate at work, this could be a sign that your testosterone levels have dropped. You may experience a sudden loss of sex drive or wake up each morning with a sense of foreboding, unable to lift your head from the pillow, let alone embrace the challenges of the day ahead.

When you do finally make it through the front door and out into the waiting world, a sense of disconnect might render you helpless. Even if you have a comfortable, interesting life with close friends and a loving family, you may still feel panicky and anxious but be unable to put your finger on why. These extended periods of existential angst can be disconcerting, so you should go for a blood test and ask your GP to check your hormone levels. Hormones regulate virtually every function in the body, so it's important not to under-estimate their significance to physical and mental well-being. If some of your hormone levels are down, your GP may be able to provide you with supplements that can help restore emotional balance. These include testosterone and dehydro-epiandrosterone (or DHEA, a hormone produced in the adrenal gland) lozenges. As well as taming unpredictable mood swings, DHEA can also improve sex drive, build muscle and bone density, sharpen memory and fight the effects of ageing. Thyro Complex capsules help regulate metabolic rate and keep thyroid levels up (the thyroid stores and produces hormones that affect the function of virtually every organ in the body). Dissolvable magnesium powder should help keep you on an even keel during the day, while the night formula will aid a peaceful night's sleep. Take a high-strength omega-3 fish-oil tablet daily to help ease those midlife aches and pains. You may want to think about visiting a psychotherapist, who will be able to assess your emotional state and come up with a lifestyle plan to complement the hormone treatment. In middle age, we need to become aware of our physiology.

How to avoid depression, boredom and hopelessness

Middle age can make us lazy – either we lose our spark and can't be bothered any more, or we slip into comfortable routines and then feel trapped. We might start to lose touch with friends, preferring instead to stay in and watch TV. Some of us become flabby, obtuse and disengaged. In short, we give up trying and become just another resentful old bore. If this sounds familiar, then you need to wake up. The middle years don't have to be like this. Remember your quest for meaning is ongoing and should take you through every age of life. Just because you have settled down doesn't mean you should give up. Midlife can be hugely rewarding and full of new opportunities; besides, you are far too young to be sliding into saggy decrepitude. Look around you – there is still so much more to do and see; so many more books to read, places to visit, languages to learn.

Middle age can hollow us out if we're not careful, but rather than filling the empty space with junk food, mindless TV and grumpy self-pity open your mind to new possibilities. Middle age is a great time to take on new challenges. If your kids are grown up, you might want to think about reconnecting with your half-forgotten pre-dad self. How have you changed? Do you still have the same interests? What makes you tick these days? Free from parental pressures, do you yearn to build something with your hands, learn an instrument or read *War and Peace*?[3] How about making contact with all the friends you lost touch with during those hectic first years of fatherhood? Once you've become reacquainted with the old you, bring the focus back to your wife. Raising children will have changed her outlook too, so you may find you have drifted apart without even realising it. Try not to feel overwhelmed by this strange new dynamic. With a bit of effort, your marriage can take on a brand-new lease of life. Remind yourselves of what you were like before the kids came along.

Divorce in middle age

If your children have left home, you and your partner may be struggling to pick up where you left off. Your focus up until now has been on raising kids, so you might not remember what it's like to be just the two of you. So much will have changed over the intervening years you may have forgotten what brought you together in the first place. Perhaps you don't even recognise the person you share a bed with any more. All those personality traits you found endearing early on in your relationship might seem stale and irritating now that perspectives and priorities have changed. If you have neglected your marriage, don't be surprised if you have nothing left to say to each other. All those parental years of transference and non-communication can easily turn to anger and resentment if left unresolved.

You may start to wonder why you are wasting precious time with someone you no longer know or even like. One or other of you might decide there is nothing left to salvage, and you'd be better off apart. Before making any rash decisions, think carefully about the long-term implications. What effect will divorce have on your children's lives? Are they secure enough to weather such a traumatic storm? Perhaps the two of you would be better off having a trial separation to allow you to gather your thoughts. Rather than feeling bitter, use this time apart to think about how you might save what's left of the relationship. Keep reminding yourself of those marriage vows: 'for richer, for poorer, in sickness and in health'; these were solemn promises you made, each one imbued with profound meaning. One of the purposes of marriage is to protect you and your children from the vagaries of uncertainty. If, after a period of reflection, you are still struggling to see a way through, then you will need to think seriously about where you go from here. But remember, divorce should only ever be a last resort, especially if you have children.

Tempus fugit

Life suddenly seems to speed up in middle age, but try not to let the passing of time trouble you too much. Midlife brings a fair amount of anxiety and regret as you watch the days and months hurtle by. There will be times, often during birthdays and New Year celebrations, when you look back wistfully at your life and wonder what might have been – this is normal. We all feel we could have done things differently if only we'd had more time. That is life's tragedy.

A note on turning forty

Few of us relish the prospect of turning forty, but why should this particular landmark fill us with such dread? According to the Office for National Statistics, average life expectancy for men in the UK stands at 79.9 in 2020, so perhaps our distress has something to do with the psychological implications of reaching a symbolic halfway mark and the realisation that we have yet to achieve many of our ambitions.[4] The sad truth is, none of us ever feels as though we have achieved enough whatever age we happen to be at. However successful we may appear, there is always more we could have done had we applied ourselves. But this is just another of life's unsolvable tragedies. Some of us take stock of our lives and feel let down. But how could it be any other way? Looking back, it's only possible to recall tiny fragments of our past, so of course life seems pitifully short and hopelessly inadequate. If by some miracle we were able to stand back and see life in its entirety, we'd be amazed at all the incredible things we have achieved. Think about it: you began life as a mewling, puking baby unable to walk, talk or control your bowel movements. Now look at you! Imagine how many twists and turns of fate it has taken to get you to where you are now.

Our fear of turning forty is often to do with perception. When we were young, the idea of being middle aged seemed preposterous and tragic. You might have pitied your forty-year-old dad, with his receding hairline, expanding waistline and terrible taste in music. And now here you are about to hit forty yourself, thinking, I hope I don't turn out like him. For all your fear and trepidation, you probably don't feel like a wobbly bellied, tone-deaf midlifer. You might even look in the mirror and be surprised by your youthful complexion and trim figure. Chances are you feel the same as you did when you turned thirty. Once you get past the interminable build-up (always the worst part), you'll wonder what all the fuss was about. You may not be partying quite as hard as you once did, you might even have slowed down physically, but you'll most likely have the consolation of a wife and family, and if you're lucky, a decent job that pays the bills. And even if you don't have all these things, you still have half your life ahead of you to make good. This in itself will seem like a blessing as you approach the next act.

Meaningful things to rediscover in middle age

- **The wonders of nature** The natural world has the power to lift us spiritually, emotionally and intellectually. Nature's beauty and diversity feeds our hunger for meaning. The lilting landscape, the changing seasons, the instincts that drive wild animals, all these wonders offer us perspective on our own lives. Next time you feel worn down by life, head to the country and marvel at the intricacy of trees, the majesty of a wind-blasted mountain, the drama of a river at high tide, the subtle beauty of insects. Nature is there for you to contemplate, interpret and enjoy. Walk amongst it, camp out in it, gaze at it, get as close to it as you can as often as you can and feel spiritually and emotionally cleansed.

- **Great works of fiction and philosophy** It would take several lifetimes to read all the classics, but that doesn't mean you shouldn't make a dent. In our youth, we are often too distracted by life to focus on reading. But now you are in the dignified middle years there really is no excuse not to enrich your mind.

- **Classic movies you may have missed** Start with Fellini and work your way through the classics.

- **Hobbies** Perhaps you think that hobbies are for children, but maintaining an interest outside work and family keeps your mind engaged.

- **New skills** Learn to cook like a pro, take up pottery, design a website, create an app, learn self-defence, practise yoga.

- **Helping others** Serving others will put your own midlife anxieties into perspective. Join a charity, volunteer at a homeless shelter, check in on elderly neighbours.

When life becomes too easy

Thankfully, few of us will have to struggle to find food or a place to sleep tonight, but when life becomes too easy, we have a tendency to lose perspective. Restlessness and dissatisfaction set in. A meaningful life takes effort, so when things fall too easily into our lap, we can feel bereft.

You probably experience the usual twenty-first-century anxieties – mortgage repayments, work–life balance, what you're going to have for dinner – but compared with the hardship that plagued previous generations (read *Down and Out in Paris and London* and *The Road to Wigan Pier* by George Orwell) your life is easy.[5] There's an old northern expression that says of the comfortably off that they 'don't know they're born'. Trouble is, when you 'don't know you're born', you don't know you're alive. In theory, we should be exceedingly grateful that we no longer have to worry about where our next meal is coming from or whether we might freeze to death, but it is only by experiencing and overcoming such hardship that we are able to appreciate the good stuff. When our needs are constantly being met, we lose sight of who we are and risk becoming over-entitled, grumpy and dissatisfied. We forget that overcoming obstacles not only gives life purpose and meaning but also offers us precious snippets of fulfilment with each battle won. Despite our fragility, we humans are remarkably resilient creatures, but every now and then we need to be reminded of that fact or else we become complacent. It may be a cliché, but many of us really do have to experience darkness in order to appreciate light.

So, if you are longing to inject some perspective into your relatively trouble-free middle-aged existence, there are little things you can do to wake you from your complacency. Next time there's a downpour, for instance, try cycling to work instead of taking the bus. By the time you arrive home, huddled and frozen to the core, you will probably feel like bursting into tears. But as you remove your sodden clothes, take comfort in the Greek philosopher Epicurus, who reminds us that real pleasure comes not from acquisition but from the removal of pain.[6] Who knew that the removal of sopping socks could elicit such intense pleasure or that a simple hot shower could feel like a sousing from God? Relish the bliss of wrapping yourself in a warm dressing gown, glass of whisky in hand, frozen extremities tingling back to life. None of these little shudders of joy would have been possible without having first put yourself through the grinder.

That yearning for perspective doesn't have to end with unpleasant bike rides. Every day, try throwing yourself in the way of some unpleasantness or other. If you live on the tenth floor of an apartment block, take the stairs instead of the lift and then repeat three times. Put off seeing a close friend for a while, or starve yourself of your favourite food for a month. Volunteer at a soup kitchen to remind yourself how lucky you are.

Clinical psychologist and psychoanalyst Dr Stephen Blumenthal understands the importance of this kind of 'forced perspective'. He sees a lot of depression and anxiety, especially in men, and believes that material and sensory abundance can have a numbing effect on the human psyche: 'When we no longer have to struggle for things, we lose motivation and our capacity for joy. Human beings need hurdles to overcome in order to keep us going.' It's also worth remembering George Bernard Shaw's advice to 'choose the line of greatest advantage rather than yielding in the direction of least resistance'; in other words, never underestimate the rewards that come with struggle.[7]

Masochism certainly isn't the road to nirvana, but there are lots of little adjustments you can make to roughen things up a bit, just enough so that you don't become numb to life's little elations. You could start by changing your eating arrangements. These days many of us eat simply out of habit, and in middle age that can mean weight gain and health issues.

Food is so plentiful that mealtimes are often simply a way to break up the monotony of the day. Ask yourself, when was the last time you felt gut-gnawingly hungry? Most of us plough through three meals a day, with plenty of snacking time in between, meaning we simply don't have time to feel hunger, which is a shame because food tastes so much more delicious when you starve yourself a little. You may be in such a hurry you forget to chew, which means you are missing out on the most pleasurable part of the eating process. Once or twice a week, try skipping breakfast or lunch or both, and you'll find that dinner is so much tastier. You will start to look forward to mealtimes rather than just going through the masticating motions. You could even take it further by fasting once a week or by drastically reducing portion size. Your enjoyment of even the humblest of food will increase dramatically. Your health will improve too.

Epicurus urged 'moderation for the maximisation of pleasure', understanding that once you strip away the excess guff, our needs are remarkably modest. And it's important to remember that all pleasure is finite; try dining out at an all-you-can-eat restaurant and see how it makes you feel.

How to stay fit in Act Five

You can't live a meaningful life if you are constantly worrying about your health. In middle age the body starts to slow down, so you need to be extra vigilant. Here's a nutrition and fitness guide designed for those entering the middle years.

Nutrition

- Be an early riser and enjoy the wonders of a dawn sunrise.

- Avoid junk food and make time to prepare your own meals using fresh Mediterranean ingredients, including plenty of green vegetables. Cooking is much simpler than you think, so don't be intimidated by cookery books.

- When you wake up, drink a large glass of water (room temperature) with lemon and ginger or turmeric powder. Stay rehydrated by drinking at least eight glasses of water a day.

- Your first meal should be thirty to forty-five minutes after you wake up.

- Don't eat too late – you will sleep better if you have supper before 7 p.m.

- Avoid fizzy drinks and sugary snacks.

- If you drink coffee, take it black (or with almond milk), without sugar and after breakfast.

- Prepare your food with coconut oil or butter. Avoid ready meals, takeaways and all processed food.

- Sleep six to eight hours (best between 11 p.m. and 7 a.m.).

- Watch your alcohol intake. In middle age, drinking to excess often makes us feel more morose than elated. Hangovers can be particularly debilitating and tend to linger for longer. Even in small measures, alcohol can cause depression, anxiety and irritability. As such, you may want to adapt your consumption accordingly, or better still give up completely. Becoming teetotal is often much easier than we think — unless you are a serious alcoholic, the body adapts remarkably quickly. Without alcohol turning your brain to mush, your life will improve no end — you'll be able to think more clearly and get many more things done.

Men over forty need to pay special attention to what they eat. Portion control is vital if you want to avoid obesity and heart attack. Your metabolic rate starts to slow with age, so shifting those extra pounds will become increasingly difficult. Muscles also start to waste away, so make sure your diet includes plenty of protein such as lean meat, nuts, pulses and eggs. After about the age of fifty, bone breakdown begins to outpace bone formation, leading to diseases such as arthritis.[8] There are more than ten million arthritis sufferers in the UK, and contrary to popular belief this horribly debilitating illness can affect people of all ages, including children.[9] To avoid painful bone conditions, make sure you include a daily dose of calcium typically found in seafood, cheese and leafy greens. You should also consider adopting a healthy plant-based diet with a daily dose of vitamins C, D and E. If you were brought up on meat and two veg, you might think vegetarianism is only for hippies, but all the evidence suggests that a meat-free Mediterranean diet can lead to a long and healthy life.

Fitness instructor Nikola Petrovac works on cruise ships, where the majority of his clients are middle aged or older. Here is an example of some of the dietary options he recommends for health–conscious midlifers.

Breakfast (choose one item each from 1, 2 and 3)

1. Eggs (fried, boiled or omelette) with vegetables; chicken salad; salmon with vegetables

2. Avocado; scoop of peanut butter; scoop of almond butter

3. Green juice (celery, ginger and cucumber); Greek yoghurt; almond milk; soya milk

Supplements: magnesium 500 milligrams + vitamin C 500 milligrams + omega-3 fish oil

Snack

Raw nuts without salt (almonds, macadamia, walnuts 50 to 100 grams) and low to medium glycaemic–index fruits (berries, mandarin, pineapple) – the best time for fruits is before, during or after a workout

Lunch (choose one item each from 1, 2 and 3)

1. Chicken breast; tuna salad; turkey breast; red meat (two times per week), grilled or boiled, not fried; white fish (cod, haddock); oily fish (mackerel, kippers); falafel

2. Vegetable salad (broccoli, asparagus, mushroom, courgette, spinach, cauliflower, lettuce, cucumber, celery, radish, aubergine, cabbage, tomato, artichoke, olives, brassica, sprouts, peppers), topped with cold-pressed oils

3. Seeds or beans; lentils; chickpeas; peas; brown rice; sweet potato

Supplements: zinc 50 milligrams

Snack

Berries with Greek yoghurt or almond milk with chai seed

Dinner (choose one item each from 1 and 2)

1. Chicken breast; turkey breast; tuna salad; tofu (lean protein only)
2. Vegetable salad (broccoli, asparagus, mushroom, courgette, spinach, cauliflower, lettuce, cucumber, celery, radish, aubergine, cabbage, tomato, artichoke, olives, brassica, sprouts, peppers), topped with cold-pressed oils

Snack

30 grams of unsalted nuts

Exercise and stretching

In middle age, your joints will start to seize up without regular exercise, so try to get into a routine – walk, run, swim or go to the gym twice a week to keep joints and muscles supple. Every morning before you go to work, try this simple but effective half-hour stretching routine:

1. Sit cross-legged with your hands on your knees, palms pointing upwards, shoulders relaxed. Close your eyes and inhale slowly through your nose and exhale from your mouth. Slowly move your head backwards and then forwards until your chin nearly touches your chest. Repeat ten times. Then

turn your head to the left and right, gently stretching your neck muscles. With your right hand, pull your head to the right and then the left.

2. Inhale, raise your right arm and stretch as far as you can to your left. Repeat ten times, then repeat with left arm. Stretch both arms out to the side then bring them in and hug your chest, stretching your back muscles. Hold for ten seconds.

3. Remaining in a cross-legged position, stretch your arms forward and try to touch the ground in front of you. Only go as far as you can and don't push too hard. Relax for fifteen seconds.

4. Straighten your legs out in front of you, inhale through your nose and lean forward until you touch your toes (if you can reach that far). Hold for thirty seconds. Shake your legs out and relax.

5. Bend your right leg in, stretch over and touch your left toes. Hold for one minute. Do the same thing on the other side, inhaling through your nose, exhaling through your mouth. Shake your legs out.

6. Spread your legs until you feel a slight tightening in your inner thighs, exhale and stretch over to your left leg. Touch your toes if you can and hold for one minute. Repeat on your right side. Relax, close your legs, raise your right knee, fold your left arm over it and stretch for one minute. Repeat on the other side.

7. Lie back and bring your right knee towards your chest. Hold for one minute and then repeat on the other side. Open your right knee and roll it over your left leg towards the floor keeping your back flat on the ground. Hold it there for one minute and repeat on the other side.

8. Lie on your left side, bend your right leg behind you, grab your right ankle and stretch. Hold for one minute and repeat on the other side.

9. Lie on your front. Push up with your arms until your chest is facing outward, stretching your lower back. Turn your head to the right and then the left. Hold for thirty seconds.

10. Sit in a kneeling position and stretch your arms out in front of you in a praying position. Hold for two minutes.

11. Rise up on your knees and lean back, stretching your lower back.

12. In a kneeling position, raise your right leg forward into a lunging position. Stretch outwards. Repeat on the other side.

13. Raise your backside in the air and make a triangular shape. Raise your right leg and move forward and push your chest out. Repeat on the other side.

14. Lie on your back. Allow your knees to relax outward towards the floor and stretch your right arm over your head. Repeat on the other side. Hold for one minute. Stretch both arms behind your head and pull your right arm with your left hand. Repeat on the other side.

15. Lie on your back and take twenty deep breaths in through your nose and out through your mouth.

A note on the trials of middle age

For a remarkable exploration of the male midlife malaise watch all three seasons of *The Fall and Rise of Reginald Perrin* by David Nobbs, first shown on the BBC in 1976.

Beating age rage

As you hit your middle years, you might start to feel alienated from the modern world. Everything is changing around you, and yet you seem to be standing still. You no longer identify with modern fashions and musical tastes; the young seem shallow and ill informed. The world no longer makes any sense. You want to yell out, but no one is listening. Indignities pile up as your looks begin to fade and women stop noticing you. The sudden realisation that you are nearer the end of life than the beginning can come as a nasty wake-up call. Fear and help-lessness slowly turn to rage; you start to blame the people closest to you, endangering your marriage and tainting friendships. Your mental and physical health may start to suffer. Most heart attacks occur in middle age as stress levels grow and blood pressure rises.

Anger can creep up on us for all sorts of reasons and in many different ways. If you are one of those people who explode at the slightest provocation, you will need to take a step back. Anger is an impulsive emotion, so you need to become aware of the space between stimulus and response. The most important thing to do when you feel the red mist descend is to stop, take a deep breath and look at the bigger picture. When you feel that familiar tightening of the chest or fluttering in the stomach, ask yourself, will it matter in five minutes? If not, let it go. Know when to walk away from potential conflicts. If an argumentative colleague is winding you up at work and you feel you're about to explode, leave the room, take some deep breaths and don't come back until the feeling has subsided. Try walking away from sticky situations before they turn ugly; anger dissipates with distance.

So much of the irritation we feel stems from the unfulfilled promise of middle age, a place where clarity was supposed to burst forth and make sense of our lives. Instead of arriving at that longed-for place of peace, many midlifers find themselves trapped in emotional turmoil. You may feel cheated and demoralised. Once you learn to control your anger you will be much better equipped to deal with life's disappointments. If middle age teaches us anything, it is that things are rarely as bad as they seem. So, whether you are leading a life of quiet desperation or seething at life's injustices, it's worth remembering ex-prime minister Arthur Balfour's wise maxim: 'Nothing matters very much and few things matter at all'.

Try these tips for beating midlife anger as recommended by anger-management guru Mike Fisher:[10]

1. Stop, breathe and take a look at the bigger picture If what's annoying you now won't matter in five minutes, it's not worth blowing up over.

2. Don't worry if you have a different opinion Try not to rail at someone for disagreeing with you – or feel shame for disagreeing with them.

3. Listen attentively Even if you disagree with someone, try to understand his or her point of view. You might actually learn something. There are always two sides to every argument.

4. Turn to people you care about Call up friends or family and talk about why you are feeling angry. This will help ease any pent-up emotions and anxieties.

5. Write it down Keep a daily journal of your moods and note when you see patterns of behaviour emerging. This will help you to identify the sorts of things that trigger those feelings of shame, fear and disconnection that can so easily tip over into fury. By charting the ebb and flow of your anger, you'll start to understand what's really upsetting your state of mind.

6. It's not always about you. Try not to take everything so personally. Life is easier if you can learn to move on quickly from a row. Most disagreements are trivial and will most likely be forgotten about by the end of the day.

7. Meditate for twenty minutes every morning Follow simple breathing exercises that will help keep you calm and centred. There are plenty of meditation/mindfulness/anti-anxiety apps available online, many of which are free.

The ageing process can be deeply frustrating and full of little annoyances, so it's important to retain a sense of humour. Physical changes can seem especially cruel. We might feel young on the inside, but outside there's no hiding from the fact that our bodies are in decline. It may be comforting to think of wrinkles and laughter lines as 'characterful', but catch them in an unflattering light and you may find yourself recoiling in horror. On the other hand, you could be one of those lucky men who become better looking with age – think George Clooney or Tom Cruise. If you have lived a healthy, meaningful life, it will more than likely show in your face and posture. Maintain a sunny, positive disposition and your eyes should keep their sparkle and those shoulders will remain firmly back.

Unfortunately, a positive outlook won't help you deal with the tricky dilemma of what to do with thinning hair. At some point you will have to decide whether to grow it out or bid a sad adieu to those last desperate wisps. Many of us opt for the 'nothing is better than something' rule and set about shaving any remaining tufts. Shorn of head hair, some will be tempted to overcompensate for the loss by growing an unwieldy beard, reverting to an 'anything is better than nothing' attitude. Those lucky enough to have held on to their hair will have to watch as shiny auburn locks turn to limp and lifeless grey. Friends will console you by saying you look 'distinguished'; women might describe you as a 'silver fox'. Rejoice in these compliments and whatever you do, don't be tempted to reach for the hair dye; it never looks natural and your friends will think you've gone mad.

As you trundle through your forties and into your fifties simple tasks such as bending over to pick up a pair of slippers will often be accompanied by a little groan of pain or sigh of exhaustion. Many of us will develop joint and back pain that if not treated may become increasingly debilitating in Act Six. You can limit such aches and pains by staying in shape and watching your weight.

Despite physical deterioration, middle age gives us a whole new perspective on life as we learn to appreciate what really matters after years of competitive striving in Acts Two and Three. You will stop caring about what other people think of you and become increasingly intolerant of their frippery. Try to look upon your middle years with wry amusement and remember to be grateful for what you have. Don't become one of those tiresome middle-aged bores who sit around all day complaining about how much better everything was 'back in the day'. Nostalgia can be stultifying and will almost certainly limit your horizons. Hold on to that child-like wonder and keep moving.

Take pride in your appearance and don't let yourself go physically

Here's how:

- Pluck rogue eyebrow, nasal and ear hair.

- Get your hair cut at least every three months and don't allow beards to become scraggly and unkempt – facial fuzz and lanky hair can be very ageing.

- Dress age appropriately. With generation gaps narrowing, knowing when to ditch youthful attire for something more appropriate can be tricky. You don't want to start dressing like an old man, but equally you should avoid keeping up with the kids. Try following these simple guidelines:

1. Make sure you own at least one decent, well-tailored suit – if you can't afford bespoke, choose high-quality fabric and a flattering fit. Spend as much as you can afford; inexpensive suits tend to look tacky. Think of it as an investment and avoid shiny material. Wearing a suit can boost your confidence and help improve your posture. Make sure you have a smart pair of shoes to match.

2. Crisp, white, fitted shirts are always flattering and go with pretty much anything.

3. Flat-fronted trousers are more becoming than pleats. Avoid baggy bums, ballooning hips and frayed cuffs and hems.

4. If you're not into fashion but want to stay presentable, choose a look and stick to it. Buy five pairs of well-cut jeans, six white shirts, four round-neck navy-blue sweaters and a couple of stylish jackets and then rotate as required. Having a readymade combo will mean you never have to worry about what to wear in the morning.

5. Choose smart, plain-coloured cotton or wool/cashmere sweaters – avoid unflattering elasticated hems and wrists. Polo necks may keep your neck warm but can look camp and outdated.

6. Leave dirty trainers, skinny jeans, grubby T-shirts and shapeless polyester tracksuits to teenagers who don't know any better. You are an adult, so start dressing like one.

7. Make sure you iron your clothes. People will notice if you look slovenly and your self-esteem will take a knock if you don't like what you see in the mirror.

8. If you haven't worn an item of clothing for more than two years, give it to a charity shop. Try not to hoard. A cluttered home equals a cluttered mind.

9. Avoid man-made fibres – they are bad for the skin and make you sweat.

10. Shower and change your underwear every day. You will feel so much fresher and more positive once you've showered and cleaned your teeth in the morning. Don't be tempted to wear pants and socks more than once. Keep to a strict hygiene routine. Wash your clothes, towels and bed linen regularly and hang them out to dry so they don't end up smelling of mildew.

Middle-age spread

As metabolic rates start to decrease you might begin to put on weight, so for the sake of your health and appearance remember to take regular exercise and don't overeat. Your partner will certainly appreciate your efforts, and remember that she will also be going through some physical changes, so be patient and non-judgemental. If you are both piling on the pounds, suggest a fitness routine that suits you both; be disciplined and try to have fun. There is something deeply disheartening about not being able to fit into beloved items of clothing, so avoid beer, sweets and doner kebabs if you want to stave off the dreaded paunch – remember, nutrient-free food is meaningless food.

Get checked out

Make sure you have a full MOT and blood test at least once a year. According to Public Health England, heart disease, stroke, cancer and respiratory disease are the leading causes of death in men over fifty.[11] Ask your GP to test for testicular and prostate cancer too, as these are particularly prevalent in middle-aged males (it's not as embarrassing as you think).

Erectile dysfunction

As you get older, you might struggle to maintain erections. As well as Viagra, there are other more long-term medications you might want to consider, such as Tadalafil tablets – talk to your GP. Try to have sex at least once a week to keep everything flowing. Intercourse is a vital part of your relationship, so do everything you can to remain physically able.

Bucket lists

Buy a Harley and drive across the USA if you've never done it before, but don't expect your life to change as a result. Think of it as a chance to see some amazing sights rather than an opportunity to escape from your life back home.

Create a man cave

Many of us need a space in which to potter and peruse. If you can't afford a shed or don't have your own garden, dedicate a spare bedroom or corner of the house just for you. Think of it as a calming refuge away from the stress of everyday life. Make the space as welcoming as you can; decorate it with beloved objects, install a decent sound system and some low lighting. Set up a workspace and a relaxation area if there is room. Hang your favourite pictures on the wall and lay a cosy, thick-pile rug underfoot. Keep your den sacred and exclusive to you.

Compare and despair

Try not to compete with your friends when it comes to job and lifestyle, and don't allow yourself to become envious if they appear to have more than you. Envy is like a poison that eats away at the soul. Most of us want to know where we stand in the pecking order, but in the end the race is only with yourself. On the subject of work, you may wake up one day to find that your new boss is significantly younger than you are. Being told what to do by someone twenty years your junior might seem humiliating, but remember that they will probably be feeling intimidated having to lord it over someone with your wisdom and experience. In time, everyone, from policemen to teachers to newsreaders, will start to look impossibly young, but that's only because you are getting older.

Seek comfort in people your own age

When the modern world seems strange and unfathomable, seek solace in your contemporaries. Skype or meet up with friends at least once a week to discuss big issues that interest you. We live in fascinating times, so engage with the world around you. Don't worry if debates become heated; it's all good brain food. Count your blessings and enjoy sharing the insights you have gained. And remember to maintain close friendships even when you are far apart – you're going to need each other in the next act.

Middle age – in summary

- Don't allow yourself to become an embittered old bore
- Be aware of your changing physiology
- Take pride in your appearance
- Try not to let disappointment turn to rage
- Avoid hair dye, ill-fitting clothes and straggly beards

- Take things as they come and keep it simple
- Take plenty of exercise
- Find spiritual succour in nature
- Most of us feel we haven't achieved enough, so don't berate yourself if life hasn't turned out the way you planned
- Don't let yourself go, either physically or mentally
- Keep expanding your mind (not your waistline), and don't lose your spark
- Maintain a healthy sex life, and don't be afraid to seek medical help if things stop working
- Nurture close friendships

Act Six
Old Age

His big manly voice turning again toward childish treble

Our first experience of age fright usually hits us in Act Five during those turbulent middle years when uncertainty about the future and past regrets can freeze us to the spot. Here in the penultimate act before the final curtain falls, the auditorium is starting to empty, and many of the anxieties that kept us awake at night are exiting stage left, 'pursued by a bear'. Realising that life is but a walking shadow full of sound and fury signifying not very much at all should come as a great relief in Act Six. The spectre of death no longer stalks us in quite the same way it did when we still had everything to live for. In the end, life may indeed signify nothing, but we still need the reassurance of knowing that our time on earth has been well spent.

After decades of worrying about whether you were good enough, rich enough, attractive enough, successful enough, popular enough, competent enough and just plain 'enough', you will gradually let go of the egotistical flagellations that kept you in a state of high alert throughout so much of your life. All those heady ambitions about the future – the dreams of making it big, of garnering respect, of making lots of money and proving your worth to a judgemental world – seems like so much noise now that you are in a position to weigh up what really mattered.

This profound period of reflection is where we discover whether we really have lived a meaningful life or if our priorities lay elsewhere. Did we make a difference or merely get by? We look back at 'our little life' soon to be 'rounded with a sleep' and wonder what on earth we were doing and what it all meant. All those things we thought would give us meaning – the foreign vacations, the exciting sexual encounters, luxury purchases, the extra hours spent on work projects – these things will barely even register as we rifle through a lifetime of memories searching for the moments that made us feel truly alive. As you contemplate the 'many parts' you have played during your seven ages, you will find yourself asking profound questions:

Did I do good in the world?

Did I live an honest life?

Did I help others?

Did I spend enough time with friends and family?

Did I place other people's needs before my own?

Did I open myself fully to the possibility of love?

Did I show enough gratitude for all the positive aspects of my life?

Did I laugh enough?

Did I seek out beauty and reject ugliness?

Did I fully appreciate the majesty and wonder of the natural world?

Did I pay enough attention to my own needs?

As you sit there in your dotage, turning over your life, will you be taking pride in the difficult choices you made or be racked with regret for all the time you wasted on unfulfilling pursuits and meaningless endeavours?

In Act One, we have the whole of life ahead of us. Everything and anything seems possible. In Act Two, the transition into adulthood weighs heavily on our innocence and easy optimism; decisions that will hugely affect the rest of our lives are made without full knowledge of the consequences. In Acts Three, Four and Five, our choices intensify as we contemplate long-term relationships, work life, the perilous middle years and whether or not to settle down. While there is still plenty of living left to do, here in Act Six, we have time to pick through the detritus of our past, searching for a coherent thread of meaning that will somehow tie the whole messy business together.

Welcoming the next generation

Some have described becoming a grandparent as akin to experiencing a kind of rebirth. Here you are in your twilight years, enjoying the excitement of a newborn baby all over again, only this time with the added benefit of accrued wisdom. Whether you are a hands-on grandparent or live on the other side of the world, you are now in a unique position to offer comfort, fun, reassurance and continuity.

There is something profoundly moving about the first time you hear your grandchild refer to you as 'Grandpa' or 'Grandad'. For decades you have been plain old 'Dad', but now that weight of responsibility has been lifted, and you can enjoy all the fun of parenthood without the stress of actually being a parent. As they move through the different stages of childhood, your grandchild will invent all sorts of adorably affectionate monikers to delight you with.

Now that you are no longer the chief carer you can afford to be a bit more relaxed when it comes to laying down the rules. While you should maintain a certain amount of discipline, think of yourself as the wise old fun-giver. Send your grandchild silly, unexpected treats to brighten up their day. If you have been asked to babysit, try mixing things up: have breakfast at dinner-time over a marathon board-gaming session; allow the little one to stay up late and bake a cake together; introduce them to some of the classic children's programmes you remember from the 1970s, such as *Sesame Street*, *Trumpton* and *The Basil Brush Show*. Entertain them with illuminating stories from your past and offer pearls of wisdom they can carry with them for the rest for their lives. Being around grandchildren is also great for your mental well-being. Whenever you visit, they will always be overjoyed to see you, and their youthful exuberance can help fight depression and ward off dementia. They might even help you to rediscover your passion for life. Now that you have reached the retirement years, which officially begin in your mid sixties, time is of the essence, so try to see your grandchildren as often as you can. You have so much to learn from each other.

A note on turning sixty-six

For men, old age officially begins at sixty-six (although this is likely to rise). Many of you will still feel like sprightly midlifers in your sixties and may struggle to believe that you have crossed a line, but according to the law you are now officially a 'senior citizen', meaning you can retire and claim a state pension. How much you receive depends on how long you've been in employment and how many years of National Insurance contributions you've made.[1] When it comes to your life savings, the economy might be in freefall, meaning a poor return on your investments. As an OAP, however, there will be plenty of other benefits and discounts coming your way. For example, anyone aged sixty-six and over can claim a winter-fuel allowance, meaning you won't have to worry about turning the heat up on a frosty night. You'll also receive a free bus pass for use on all off-peak journeys. Senior rail cards are available to anyone over sixty, giving one-third off standard and first-class fares. You'll even receive a one-off, tax-free £10 payment known as the 'Christmas Bonus', while all NHS prescriptions are now free. Once you hit sixty, you'll be offered discounts of up to 20 per cent at cinemas, theatres, art galleries and museums.

Retirement

However much you enjoy your job, there will come a time when you need to slow down. After years of working your way up the corporate ladder, retirement can feel like a step backwards, but there is plenty of meaning to be had outside office life. For those worried about a loss of income, the state pension provides a safety net, although this probably won't be enough to live on without additional savings. Removing yourself from the nine-to-five daily grind may come as a shock at first, but like every act of life, how you choose to spend your time will ultimately determine whether your retirement has meaning or not. The next few years will be about slowing down rather than stopping completely. As long as you remain active, the world still has plenty of meaning left for you to explore.

Now is the time to start enjoying that nest egg you've been saving for a rainy day. Of course, you will want to leave an inheritance for your grandchildren, but don't forget to save some for yourself. After all those years of hard slog, you deserve a bit of pampering. For a while you might just feel like doing nothing – lie-ins, long lunches and having time to contemplate the world around you will seem like a welcome luxury after all those years of rushing around. When the novelty eventually wears off, you will need to have a plan of action in place. Rather than being a prelude to the end, retirement might turn out be the most meaningful age of your life.

Preparing emotionally for retirement

Retirement involves some major readjustments, both monetarily and psychologically. Some will look forward to the chance to unwind, while others may feel they are losing an important part of their identity. Perhaps you already have financial arrangements in place and a perfect hideaway by the sea to move into, but one thing you may not have planned for is what to do with all that extra free time.

For years your life has been about dressing appropriately for the office, sticking to schedules and attending meetings, and now here you are in your pyjamas at 3 p.m., sipping a glass of wine, thinking, Is that it? If this is the case, you will need to start planning for the future; after all, you could live for another thirty years. Retirees often find they have more time but less money, so you may need to tighten your belt accordingly. Decide what's most important and then cut back on all the extraneous stuff. You'll have to make some difficult choices, so try not to become too overwhelmed. If you start to experience mental-health issues, such as depression or anxiety, don't suffer in silence – seek help, but also make sure you stay in touch with friends and family.

As you adapt to a slower pace of life, you will experience a whole range of different emotions. There will be times when you feel disconnected from the outside world; boredom and despair may set in as you ponder your future. You might even feel guilty because you are not enjoying retirement as much as you hoped. Keep expectations in check and remember that nothing in life is ever as good or as bad as we imagine. To break the monotony, it's important to have things to look forward to.

When you were working, you probably had a strict routine: rise at 8 a.m., shower, breakfast, go to work, come home, make supper, go to bed. You might find you are missing the comfort and security of a busy schedule, so build your own daily routine that you can stick to at home. If you are a morning person, continue setting your alarm for 7.30 a.m. and then begin your day with a few stretching exercises to ease you back to life. You could structure the rest of the day around mealtimes, as you probably did when you were working, then set aside slots for enjoyable/meaningful activities throughout the day. Don't be too rigid when it comes to timings – after all, you are your own boss now – but setting yourself goals will give you something to work towards. Think medium to long term: write down things you would like to achieve in the first six months of your retirement. Begin small: maybe you've been meaning to lose a few pounds or have ambitions to cultivate a vegetable garden. Make a start on your memoirs or family tree, and reward yourself with a treat at the end of each week.

At work, you used to run into the same people every day.

Not having that social interaction might come us a shock, but being on your own doesn't mean you have to become isolated. An active social life is harder to maintain during retirement, so make coffee mornings and dinner dates a regular part of your new routine. If going out becomes an issue, take advantage of technology and arrange to meet friends in the virtual world via Skype or Zoom.

Just because you have officially retired doesn't mean you have to leave the world of work entirely. If you were a work-aholic as a younger man, maintaining some kind of employment could be good for your mental health. You might want to think about applying for a part-time job locally. If you feel nervous about returning to a noisy, stressful office, there's plenty of meaningful work you can do from home, or you could volun-teer at a local charity.

Coming to terms with old age

When we are young, we tend to look upon old age with fear and trepidation. We struggle to understand how anyone could bear to continue living knowing that the end is in sight. But something kicks in when we enter the final acts: outlooks shift, and we become more philosophical about mortality. Perhaps we feel there is nothing left to see, do or learn and that life has simply run its course. But there is always more to life than we think. We must never become complacent and should keep on striving for purpose and meaning however old we are on paper.

Epicurus and the meaningful life

The Greek philosopher Epicurus (341–270BC) encouraged his many followers to find meaning in simple pleasures, while warning them about the dangers of overindulgence. 'Do not spoil what you have,' he wrote, 'by desiring what you have not; remember that what you now have was once among the things you only hoped for.' When it comes to food, for instance, he recommends plain, simple fare served in small portions, not because lots of fancy food is intrinsically bad, but because it increases our expectations. This in turn leads to unrealistic levels of desire, ending with disappointment.

Throughout his teachings, Epicurus reminds us that 'he who is not satisfied with a little is satisfied with nothing'. Being aware of how different pleasures make us feel and behave allows us to temper and recalibrate our desires accordingly, meaning we can avoid the sorts of pleasures that lead to anxiety and dissatisfaction. When we were young, we tended to focus on physical stimuli, dismissing as insignificant more profound pleasures such as a dramatic sunrise, a fascinating conversation with a friend or the sound of a skylark at dusk, pleasures that some of us only really start to appreciate here in the calmer waters of old age. And for those of us in our dotage who might be worrying about what happens next, Epicurus reminds us that 'death is nothing. When we exist, death is not; and when death exists, we are not. All sensation and consciousness ends with death, and therefore in death there is neither pleasure nor pain. The fear of death arises from the belief that in death, there is awareness.' Epicureanism encourages us to celebrate the here and now, something we should all be doing more of in later life when nostalgia can come to dominate our thoughts. Resisting the urge to go beyond what is necessary or what is good is based on thousands of years of human trial and error.

The Epicurean philosophy encourages us to live life to the

best of our abilities, while Epicurus himself believed passionately that a good and meaningful life was within everybody's grasp. In the 'Tetrapharmakos', his four-part remedy for anxiety and existential dread, Epicurus encourages us not to fear the gods or worry about death, consoling us with the idea that 'what is good is easy to get' — because the ultimate pleasure is the removal of pain — and 'what is terrible is easy to endure' — because most pain is short-lived and we shouldn't therefore worry about it unnecessarily.

Epicureanism isn't about running away or hiding from the world — it's about enjoying the sheer, unadulterated pleasure of living; it's about the world as it actually is, and it's about us as we truly are. Tranquillity and freedom from fear are seen as the ultimate pleasures, but they can only be achieved through knowledge, philosophy, friendship and living a good life. Epicurus reminds us that 'of all the means to insure happiness throughout the whole of life, by far the most important is the acquisition of friends'. Act Six can be an especially lonely place, so take heed.

If Epicurus's philosophy strikes a chord and you decide to live by his teachings, you'll be following in the footsteps of esteemed poets, writers, political leaders and philosophers such as Christopher Hitchens, Horace (whose phrase '*carpe diem*' — seize the day — illustrates the philosophy), Julius Caesar and founding father and president of the United States of America Thomas Jefferson.

Coping with the death of friends

The sudden loss of a close friend in Act Three would most likely devastate us, whereas in Act Six that same death won't have quite the same traumatic resonance. When we are young, death seems like a distant, unfathomable effrontery, which is why losing a friend can seem so earth shattering. Here in Act Six, we have become almost accustomed, if not resigned, to the idea of mortality – 'not so much saddening as sobering' as one eighty-three year old put it when describing the death of a cherished friend. In old age we start to lose the people we hold most dear. Many of us will have to cope with the death of a spouse or sibling. One by one, friends of fifty or sixty years' standing will start to leave us, and we will have to cope as best we can. As illness and decay sets in, hospitals become our second homes, doctors and nurses our new best friends. If you happen to be the youngest of your peer group, you might be the last man standing, which you will look upon as either a blessing or a curse.

If you have yet to reach Act Six, you may be wondering why anyone would choose to put themselves through such agony; better surely just to end it all before decrepitude sets in. Everyone who has ever made it to a great age has wondered the same thing. Nobody wants to be a burden to family or state, and none of us relishes a future dominated by slow, painful decline. A short injection and a long sleep must surely be preferable, or so you might think. Author of *Man's Search for Meaning*, Viktor Frankl writes, 'If there is a meaning in life at all, then there must be a meaning in suffering. Suffering is an ineradicable part of life, even as fate and death. Without suffering and death, human life cannot be complete.'[2] And it is this need for completion – to experience life in its entirety in the hope that meaning might finally reveal itself to us – that drives us on. Life, however undignified, will always be preferable to the unknowability of what is to come. Touchingly, many of us will continue to delude ourselves into thinking that we can some-how cheat death, that for us the end will be different, less final, less deadly. At the same time, we become more circumspect; with death now so much a part of life, pragmatism takes over and the end no longer has the power to shock.

Preparing for the end

Death is rarely discussed in our youth–obsessed culture. Even when faced with our own mortality, we tend to skirt around the issue. Here in Act Six we can no longer afford to hide from the truth. It's time to remove the blinkers, cut through the fear and look death square in the eye.

Tragically, few of us will have the luxury of dying peacefully in our sleep.[3] For many, the end will be a gruelling, drawn out affair. For those aged sixty-five and over, the most common causes of death are heart disease, cancer and chronic obstructive lung disease. Death from 'natural causes' – when malfunctioning internal organs stop working – include old age, heart attack, stroke or chronic infection, although, surprisingly perhaps, cancer is considered an 'unnatural' cause – i.e., death by active intervention from outside forces.[4] All these illnesses can leave us incapacitated and in great pain, so it's important to know the facts so you can prepare yourself for the worst.

- In the UK in 2015–2017, on average each year more than 53 per cent of deaths from cancer were in people aged seventy-five and over (according to Cancer Research UK). The disease itself might last for several years or could take you down within a few days, depend-ing on the virulence.[5]

- Of the 30,000 out-of-hospital cardiac arrests in the UK every year, the survival rate is thought to be as low as 10 per cent.

- There are around 35,000 lung-cancer deaths in the UK every year; that's ninety-seven every day (2015–2017). This particularly virulent form of the disease is the most common cause of cancer death in the UK, accounting for 21 per cent of all cancer deaths in 2017.[6]

You can help prevent these common causes of death in later life by eating less sugar and fat. You should also give up smoking if you want to avoid lung disease and only drink alcohol in moderation. Stick to these simple rules and death may look kindly upon you. As we near the end, it's also important to keep our affairs in order. Make sure your will is up to date and has been signed by a solicitor. Check that you have a power of attorney in place, and if you have decided you'd prefer to die naturally, you will need to sign a legally binding do-not-resuscitate order.

Body and mind

In old age, it's important not to fall into a sedentary life. Keep mind and body active if you want your final years to be productive, worthwhile and relatively pain free. Joints and muscles are less likely to seize up if you keep them moving. Walk for at least half an hour a day. The brain is also like a muscle that needs to be kept supple.[7] You could lessen your chances of developing dementia, for example, by engaging in daily crossword puzzles or sudoku. Try to read a book a week, and learn some of your favourite poems off by heart to keep those cognitive skills ticking over. Age may have slowed you down, but it's vital not to come to a complete standstill.

Beating loneliness

Most of us will experience two types of loneliness during our lifetime. You will recognise the big existential 'L' as that gnawing, implacable sense that we are naught but drifting atoms caught in the aloneness of our own consciousness. The terror of knowing that we are essentially alone in the universe stalks us at every age, so you had better make your peace with it early on. The other, more visceral kind of loneliness is particularly prevalent amongst older people who may feel they have been forgotten about. The fear that we no longer matter or even properly exist can send us into a spiral of despair.

The fracturing of families has only compounded what many see as a growing epidemic of loneliness. Up until relatively recently, generations tended to stick together in tightly knit communities, with children, parents and grandparents often sharing the same house, with extended family living close by. Care homes were only ever a last resort. These days offspring tend to go where the work is, meaning families are often spread across counties, countries and even continents. Those left behind have to fend for themselves.

According to the Campaign to End Loneliness, living alone and poor social connections are as bad for our health as smoking fifteen cigarettes a day. The same study found that loneliness can be worse for us than obesity. Lonely people are more likely to suffer from dementia, heart disease and depression. Isolation can increase our risk of death by 29 per cent.[8] Even for those in middle age, loneliness is turning into an epidemic, with the number of over fifties experiencing loneliness set to reach two million by 2025–26. This compares to around 1.4 million in 2016–17 – a 49 per cent increase in ten years.[9] According to Age UK there are around 1.2 million chronically lonely older people in Britain, with around half a million going at least five or six days a week without seeing or speaking to another person.[10] More than 51 per cent of all people aged seventy-five and over live alone,[11] while two-fifths (about 3.9 million) confess that television is their main source of company.[12] There are more than 2.2 million people aged seventy-five and over living alone in Britain, an increase of almost a quarter (24 per cent) over the past twenty years.[13]

According to the advice and support service Independent Age, isolation and loneliness is an emerging crisis particularly affecting older males. The number of men aged sixty-five and over living alone is projected to rise by 65 per cent between now and 2030; that's a rise from 911,000 to 1.5 million. Because older men are more socially isolated and have significantly less contact with children, family and friends, Independent Age recommends that as we approach later life we must try to retain and build our social network.[14] Authorities can help by providing more befriending and support services designed with older men's interests in mind. We should be doing far more to identify older people who are potentially most at risk of social isolation.

In our youth-orientated culture, old age is often viewed as shameful or embarrassing. Like many older people, you will be anxious not to become a burden or feel that you are imposing in any way. But this 'mustn't grumble' attitude can lead to terrible isolation. Rather than sinking into obscurity do everything you can to remind the world that you still exist and that you still matter.

Remain in contact

Don't rely on anyone to make the first move, not even your family. If your spouse has already died and you live on your own, you might feel like retreating from the world entirely, but this may prove to be your downfall. Too many old people die alone in their homes, often remaining undiscovered for days or even weeks simply because they have lost contact with the outside world. We've all heard the tragic stories. So even if your children live on the other side of the world, call them regularly for a chat and don't for a moment think that you are imposing. They will more likely than not be thrilled to hear from you. If loneliness has you in its grip, don't give in to hopelessness. Get involved with community life as much as you can. As an older citizen, you have plenty to offer. So don't keep all that accumulated wisdom to yourself, and don't sit there waiting for life to come to you.

A note to younger readers

Claiming you are too busy is not a good enough excuse to abandon your elderly relatives. If you don't make an effort now, you will regret it once they're gone. In between regular visits (put some dates in your diary right now), call them at least twice a week. Reminisce about the past, tell them an amusing anecdote or two and let them know what you've been up to. Remind them how much they mean to you and tell them not to worry. Send them a chatty, handwritten letter if you can't be there in person (it makes a refreshing change from all that junk mail they receive). Appreciate all the things your parents have done for you over the years, and show them the gratitude and respect they deserve. They may not tell you to your face, but they will be missing you, so visit as often as you can for their sake, and remember that putting other people's needs before your own is one of the most rewarding ways to live a meaningful life. Make sure you get to know their neighbours and pass on your contact details in case of emergencies.

Most aged relatives will want to retain their independence for as long as possible, but when they do become too frail to look after themselves, try to find an alternative to putting them in a home. If they need twenty-four hour care, then of course you will have to take appropriate action – do your research and choose a nursing home with friendly staff and an established reputation. Here in the UK we can be quite cavalier about our old folk, so instead of handing over responsibility to a third party, do everything you can to welcome them into your home. If you or your siblings have a spare room or a 'granny flat', think about how you might accommodate an aged parent. There will be adjustments, of course, and you will need to adapt your home accordingly (raising loo seats, and installing steady bars and stair-lifts where necessary). Because they value their independence, you might meet with some resistance. Try to reassure them that the move might only have to be temporary. Looking after an elderly parent will be hard work but hugely rewarding. Remember that meaning is found through the adoption of responsibility, and what could be more responsible than caring for a vulnerable loved one.

Bereavement

If your spouse dies before you, you will want to seek solace in your family. Go and stay with your children for as long as it takes. After a period of mourning, you'll need to start adjusting to your new life. When you do eventually return home, everything will feel different yet strangely the same. The marital home will seem eerily quiet and hollowed out. If your wife died suddenly, it will be as though a clock has stopped. Everything will be just as she left it: a pair of slippers placed neatly at the end of the bed; the imprint of her head might still be visible on the pillow. These poignant reminders will tear at your heartstrings, and for a while you may struggle to believe that she's actually gone. Don't be surprised if you find yourself waiting patiently for her to come home. This foggy sense of unreality punctuated by stabs of devastation will permeate the weeks and months ahead. Everything will remind you of your beloved, and her spirit will remain embedded in the fabric of your life. We all handle grief differently, but a few counselling sessions might be helpful.

At some point, you will need to gather your strength and go through her possessions. This will be an intensely emotional undertaking, so make sure your children are there to help. Clothes and shoes will seem especially poignant, so expect plenty of tears and mournful reminiscences. Regarding practicalities, you may have come to rely on your wife's domestic skills and find the bewildering array of household appliances daunting. The next few months will be a difficult learning curve, both practically and emotionally, but as you start to regain your independence, the pain of loss will gradually subside and you may even discover a new, rejuvenated you.

A note from Arthur Schopenhauer

'Mostly it is loss which teaches us about the worth of things.'[15]

Decluttering

At some point, you will want to have a major clear out. Sorting through a lifetime of personal effects can trigger all sorts of emotions, some happy others touching or sad. You may struggle to part with the detritus that has followed you around for so long, but it's important not to become too attached to possessions that are long past their sell-by date. You might feel guilty or even traumatised by the thought of throwing away broken appliances, mismatched china and half remembered electrical cords, but don't allow the residue of your past to clutter what's left of the future. Be ruthless; hold on to valuables and anything with genuine sentimental value. Take photographs of any newspaper cuttings you want to keep. Everything else can go. Once you've taken the plunge, it will be as though a great weight has been lifted from your shoulders and you will have done your children a great service. Finally, you will be able to locate all those things that really matter without having to rifle through piles of anxiety-inducing tat.

Watch out for scammers

Shameless con artists tend to target the old and vulnerable, using all kinds of devious methods to get their hands on your money. Anyone still using a landline, for instance, will be particularly at risk from scammers and cold callers trying to sell you things that don't exist or that you don't need. Never give out your bank details to anyone over the phone unless you have called them first to pay for a specific product or service. Be equally vigilant if anyone knocks on your front door claiming to be from the council, health authority or utility company. They might ask to come in to check for a 'gas leak' or 'subsidence'. If they try to sell you miracle cures or secondary glazing, politely ask them to leave. Make sure you have a safety lock installed and ask for ID before letting anyone in.

In old age you will also start receiving countless catalogues through your letterbox filled with overpriced products that companies struggle to sell elsewhere. Publishers of these patronising tomes assume old people are wealthy and gullible, so don't be taken in by their ludicrous over-priced gadgets such as walking frames with slipper attachments and bed-socks that double as hot-water bottles. Recycle all junk mail and notify your postman. If you do need to buy something useful but don't have access to the internet, ask one of your children to buy it for you online – it is bound to be cheaper than a catalogue equivalent. If checking email avoid opening messages from people or companies you don't recognise and never click on rogue links – if you do, you risk giving away personal details that scam artists then use to empty your account or pass on to other criminals.

Nothing to fear

It's completely natural to be anxious about death, but consider the alternative – would you really want to live for ever? Stay active, keep laughing, have regular check-ups, and try not to become too obstinate or set in your ways. When your time is up, bow out with dignity and gratitude.

A note from Anaïs Nin

'People living deeply have no fear of death.'[16]

Old age – in summary

- Don't become isolated – pick up the phone or use the internet if mobility is an issue
- Stay in touch with family and friends
- Don't hoard – everything has a sell-by date, so don't be afraid to let go of unnecessary detritus. When decluttering, be ruthless and only hold on to things that have genuine sentimental value
- If your body starts to fail, don't give in to bitterness
- Enjoy your retirement years and learn to adjust to changing circumstances
- Remain open-minded and inquisitive
- Don't become obstinate or set in your ways
- Make plans and give yourself things to look forward to
- Stay engaged and keep mobile
- Follow Epicurus's teachings – enjoy the simple life, and don't worry about death
- Don't give up on life if your spouse dies before you
- Loneliness is a killer
- Death is a law not a punishment

Act Seven
Death and Legacy

Sans teeth, sans eyes, sans taste, sans everything

O me! O life! of the questions of these recurring,
Of the endless trains of the faithless, of cities
    fill'd with the foolish,
Of myself forever reproaching myself, (for who
    more foolish than I, and who more faithless?)
Of eyes that vainly crave the light, of the objects
    mean, of the struggle ever renew'd,
Of the poor results of all, of the plodding and
    sordid crowds I see around me,
Of the empty and useless years of the rest,
    with the rest me intertwined,
The question, O me! so sad, recurring –
    What good amid these, O me, O life?

Answer.

    That you are here – that life exists and identity,
    That the powerful play goes on, and you may contribute a verse.

'O Me! O Life!'
Walt Whitman[1]

The final curtain

A remarkable Australian nurse named Bronnie Ware spent several years of her life working in palliative care, nursing patients as they lived out the final twelve weeks of their lives. In her blog 'Inspiration and Chai', she recorded their dying epiphanies and the exceptional clarity of vision they displayed as they faced their own mortality. 'When questioned about any regrets they had or anything they would do differently,' she writes, 'common themes surfaced again and again.' These included wishing they had been truer to themselves, wishing they'd had the courage to express their feelings more openly, wishing they'd stayed in touch with friends and wishing they'd allowed themselves to be happier.[2]

One of the most common regrets of the men in her care was wishing that they hadn't worked so hard, which is surprising when you consider how much importance we place on work in Acts Three, Four and Five. Perhaps if we had focused our attention on meaningful employment, we might not have minded the heavy workload – 90,000 hours is a lot of life to feel regretful about.

For younger readers, try to imagine what sort of regrets you might have in your seventh age based on the sort of person you are now and then consider how you might pre-empt them in Acts Three, Four and Five.

Ask yourself these pertinent questions:

- Are you being true to yourself and authentic with others?

- Are you mindful of all those little kindnesses you could be showing to people around you?

- Is there an elderly neighbour you could be checking up on? (Go and knock on their door right now and offer to do some shopping. Make them a cup of tea and stay for a chat.) Perhaps there's a homeless man on your street in need of a blanket, some warming soup and a few reassuring words. Knowing that you helped your fellow man will remain with you until the end.

- What about your tendency to procrastinate? Might that be something you are going to regret in later life?

- Are you telling the people you care about how much you love them?

- Is putting up with other people's bad behaviour going to be something you ruminate upon in old age?

- What about that road trip across America you've been promising yourself? Do it now while you still can.

- Do you long to move to the country?

- Are you surrounding yourself with beauty? (Don't waste precious time on ugliness.)

- Is there a wrong that needs righting, an ex-friend to make peace with, an estranged mother to forgive?

Muster your powers of compassion and clear the decks of all those future regrets. Do it now, because someday never comes.

A note from the Dalai Lama

When asked what surprised him most about humanity, the Dalai Lama answered, 'Man. Because he sacrifices his health in order to make money. Then he sacrifices money to recuperate his health. And then he is so anxious about the future that he does not enjoy the present; the result being that he does not live in the present or the future; he lives as if he is never going to die, and then dies having never really lived.'[3] It's a sobering observation and one we should all take on board so that we never have to wonder why we never really lived.

The gift of foresight

Having foresight includes knowing what to prioritise as meaningful early on. Founder of the Boy Scout movement Robert Baden-Powell had this advice for young men starting out in life: 'Try and leave this world a little better than you found it, and when your turn comes to die, you can die happy in feeling that at any rate you have not wasted your time but have done your best.'[4]

Legacy

What do you want your life to stand for? As we approach the end, many of us will worry about our legacy. We want the world to know that we were here and that we mattered. For most of us, however, the vapour trail of our existence will dissolve remarkably quickly, leaving virtually no trace. How many of us, for instance, know much about our great-grandparents' lives? Go back three or four generations and predecessors are little more than strangers in faded photographs, however much they may have achieved in their lifetimes.

The chances are no one will remember you beyond your immediate friends and family, and once they are gone you too will become just another stranger in a digital photograph. If that sounds depressing, take comfort in the fact that even Nobel Peace prize-winners and world-renowned philanthropists will be shorn of significance once their flame has burnt out. The best we can hope for is to be able to look back on our lives and hope that we are leaving the world a better person than when we arrived.

Give the gift of legacy

Your own legacy may be gone within a couple of generations, but there is something you can do to keep a loved one's memory alive, digitally at least. Many children regret not having anything tangible to remember parents by other than a few photographs and a box of dog-eared letters. But this can easily be remedied and with profound consequences. All you need is an elderly relative, a smartphone with a decent video camera and a list of questions. Seat your subject in a comfortable armchair, roll the camera and contribute to their legacy by allowing them to tell their story. Once they are sufficiently relaxed, ask probing questions that future generations will find revealing. If you choose to make a recording of your elderly father, for instance, imagine you are meeting him for the first time and start by asking him about his childhood. Did he have a strict upbringing? Were his parents affectionate towards him? Was he a contented young man? What were his ambitions? Is he happy with the way his life turned out? What five things would he change if he could start over again? Does he have any regrets or frustrated ambitions? What does he think about modern masculinity? Which are the qualities he most admires in other men? Ask him about his marriage and if he has any advice for those thinking of settling down. What are his thoughts on religion, politics, sex and fatherhood? Does he have any parenting tips? What life lessons would he like to pass on to future generations? Is he afraid of death? What is his definition of a meaningful life?

You might want to think about making a series of recordings over a number of years so you can see how his attitude changes over time. These insightful vignettes could be an invaluable history lesson, connecting future generations with the wisdom of blood relatives. The power of digital technology means that hundreds of years from now, distant descendants in the future could conceivably have access to high-definition footage of how we live today. It would be the equivalent of us watching crystal-clear interviews with our medieval ancestors, the wisdom of generations gifted to us through the ages.

The end

So here you are. Congratulations. You made it to the final act. You have had your exits and your entrances, and in your time have played many parts. As you look back on your uniquely remarkable life and contemplate shuffling off this mortal coil, think long and hard about what impact you have had on the people around you. How has the world been a better place with you in it? What contributions have you made through your work? Whose lives have you touched? Are there any lessons you would like to hand on to future generations? What do you want to leave behind?

Your ability to accept death will very much depend on whether you feel your time on earth has been well spent. If your three score and ten has lacked purpose, you may find yourself raging against the dying of the light; if you wasted your life on trivialities and pleasures of the flesh, you may long for a chance to go back and start again; if your life has remained unexamined, you may wonder whether it was worth living. Did you allow yourself to be inexorably drawn to life's unfulfilling shallow end, or did you dare to dive deeper? In the words of Mark Twain, 'A man who lives fully is prepared to die at any time.'

Our revels now are ended. These our actors,
As I foretold you, were all spirits and
Are melted into air, into thin air:
And, like the baseless fabric of this vision,
The cloud-capp'd towers, the gorgeous palaces,
The solemn temples, the great globe itself,
Yea, all which it inherit, shall dissolve
And, like this insubstantial pageant faded,
Leave not a rack behind. We are such stuff
As dreams are made on, and our little life
Is rounded with a sleep.

The Tempest, Act IV, Scene I
William Shakespeare

A note from Emily Dickinson

'That it will never come again is what makes life so sweet.'[5]

Conclusion

The world is changing in unimaginable ways, and yet despite the turmoil our hunger for meaning continues. In times of dramatic flux, through wars and pandemics, our very survival depends on a willingness to come together and cooperate. If we are to grow and develop as a species, we have no choice but to see beyond petty jealousies, tribal allegiances, toxic rivalries and our narcissistic need for control. As a nation we have to decide what sort of society we want to live in.

Looking to an uncertain future, there has never been a more pressing need for meaningful connection. The time has come to reject greedy self-interest and return to first principles by embracing what we already know in our hearts to be true. Only then can we start to rebuild trust in one another and have faith in those institutions designed to foster our better natures.

Let's take this opportunity to learn from past mistakes. We need to put aside all those political and cultural doctrines that have divided us for so long. Instead of returning to tired old orthodoxies, we should focus on improving the lives of those we are most responsible for – our spouses, work colleagues, aged parents, friends, that lonely old woman across the street. Rather than blaming others for the desperate state of the world, we should look to ourselves and ask how we can become kinder, more responsible citizens. Worrying about things we cannot realistically change and hankering after Utopian fantasies won't make the world a better place.

We need to start judging everyone we meet on his or her individual merits and try to live by example. Foster deep connections, show gratitude, moral courage, humility and forgiveness, find a meaningful job, get married, raise a family, serve your local community, nurture your better nature and always do the decent thing by putting other people's needs before your own.

Now, if each one of us could make a vow to do all that, the world really would be a more meaningful place.

How to live a meaningful life – in summary

- Adopt responsibility
- Find fulfilment in the service of others
- Seek out beauty and turn your back on ugliness
- Find purpose through meaningful work
- Embrace love. Form deep connections. Get married and have children. The nuclear family is the glue holding society together
- Embrace decency, good manners and a strong moral framework
- Show good faith when dealing with others
- Cherish friendships
- Honour your better nature
- Be strong and dependable when you need to be, but don't be afraid to open up emotionally

- Celebrate our common humanity
- Don't be ashamed of traditional masculinity. Strength, resilience, stoicism and ambition have served men well throughout history. Abandon them at your peril
- Treat everyone you meet as a unique individual capable of good and evil. Always give them the benefit of the doubt and judge them purely on the content of their character
- Enjoy the simple life and learn to live with less. Life is fleeting, so cherish what you have and don't get bogged down by the lure of material acquisition
- Avoid shallow pleasures. Instant gratification can lead to long-term dissatisfaction. Stay away from coarse popular culture – it is designed to appeal to your baser instincts
- Join a charity. Work in a soup kitchen. Help the homeless. Help the aged. Do what you can. Treat others as you would like to be treated
- Show gratitude, forgiveness and grace

How to be a meaningful man – a summary

- Be emotional but don't be ruled by your emotions
- Be vulnerable but don't be weakened by your vulnerability
- Be tough when you feel scared
- Be brave if you want to get things done
- Be resolute when faced with a challenge
- Be stoical when life is getting you down

- Be resilient if you want to survive
- Be ambitious if you want to get to the top
- Be competent if you want to stay on top
- Be generous if you want to be liked
- Be chivalrous if you want her to stick around
- Be protective if you want your children to respect you
- Be a perfectionist if you want to be the best
- Be decisive if you want to make progress
- Be confident if you want to change the world
- Be a risk taker if you really believe in something
- Be self-reliant for when the world comes crashing around your ears
- Be motivated if you want to better yourself
- Be a non-conformist if you want to be true to yourself
- Be good to your body if you want to live a healthy life
- Be hungry for knowledge if you want to understand the world around you
- Be a leader if you think you have what it takes
- Be responsible if you want people to respect you
- Be your own man and don't let others push you around if you value your self-esteem
- Be prepared to listen to others but speak out if you think they're wrong
- Be dutiful if you want to earn the respect of others
- Be prepared to ring the Samaritans if you feel you can't go on
- Be more than just your gender – be you!
- . . . be all these things, and you'll be a man, my son.

All the world's a stage,
And all the men and women merely players;
They have their exits and their entrances;
And one man in his time plays many parts,
His acts being seven ages. At first the infant,
Mewling and puking in the nurse's arms;
And then the whining school-boy, with his satchel
And shining morning face, creeping like snail
Unwillingly to school. And then the lover,
Sighing like furnace, with a woeful ballad
Made to his mistress' eyebrow. Then a soldier,
Full of strange oaths, and bearded like the pard,
Jealous in honour, sudden and quick in quarrel,
Seeking the bubble reputation
Even in the cannon's mouth. And then the justice,
In fair round belly with good capon lin'd,
With eyes severe and beard of formal cut,
Full of wise saws and modern instances;
And so he plays his part. The sixth age shifts
Into the lean and slipper'd pantaloon,
With spectacles on nose and pouch on side;
His youthful hose, well sav'd, a world too wide
For his shrunk shank; and his big manly voice,
Turning again toward childish treble, pipes
And whistles in his sound. Last scene of all,
That ends this strange eventful history,
Is second childishness and mere oblivion;
Sans teeth, sans eyes, sans taste, sans everything.

As You Like It, Act II, Scene VII
William Shakespeare

Acknowledgements

I would like to thank my editors Andreas Campomar and Claire Chesser for all their gentle encouragement and wise prodding throughout the various stages of this book. Thanks also to the dynamic team at Little, Brown and Hachette – Tim Whiting, Beth Wright, Aimee Kitson, John Fairweather and Matthew Burne – and to Paul Murphy for line-editing duties. I am indebted to my delightful agent Matthew Hamilton at The Hamilton Agency for believing in the project from the start and for knocking ideas into shape (thank you esteemed members of the rock band Yes for inadvertently bringing us together). I am grateful to the eminent clinical psychologist and psychoanalyst Dr Stephen Blumenthal for all his insights and expertise, and to the many men and women who have opened up to me about their longings, desires, insecurities and regrets – you have helped me understand what makes us all tick. Finally, I'd like to send love and gratitude to my wife Anna for all her kindness and patient understanding; you have shown me what it means to live a meaningful life.

Endnotes

A Brief History of Modern Man

1   'Notes on the English Character' essay, E. M. Forster, 1926.

2   'The End of Men', Hanna Rosin, *The Atlantic*, 15 August 2010.

3   'Out of sight, out of mind: why less well-off, middle-aged men don't get the support they need', The Samaritans, 2012.

4   Times Up, a movement against sexual harassment, founded 1 January 2018, by Hollywood celebrities in response to the Weinstein scandal and #MeToo.

5   Me Too, a movement to support victims of sexual violence, was founded in 2006 by Tarana Burke.

Childhood

1   *The Boy Crisis: Why Our Boys Are Struggling and What We Can Do About It*, Warren Farrell, BenBella Books, 2018.

2   Annual report from Relationships Foundation, a think tank for a better connected society.

3   'Child Poverty in Perspective: An Overview of Child Well-being in Rich Countries', The United Nations Children's Fund, 2007. A comprehensive assessment of the lives and well-being of children and adolescents in the economically advanced nations.

4   'Dying to Be Young: An in-depth review of street gangs in Britain', The Centre for Social Justice, February 2009. A policy report by the Gangs Working Group, Chaired by Simon Antrobus.

5   Study by clinical psychologist Jenny Taylor cited in 'Crime linked to absent fathers', Sarah Hall, *Guardian*, 5 April 2001.

6   Belinda Brown and Men for Tomorrow cited in 'The women demonised for championing men's rights: They devote their lives to a deeply unfashionable cause – helping "downtrodden" men in the age of gender politics. And they've provoked a bitter divide', James Innes-Smith, *Daily Mail*, 27 November 2019.

7   Reference to Sheldon Thomas in 'David Lammy MP says absent fathers "key cause of knife crime"', BBC News website, 3 October 2012.

8   'Dad and Me – Research into the Problems Caused by Absent Fathers', Martin Glynn and Addaction, 2011.

9   *Social Problems in a Free Society: Myths, Absurdities, and Realities*, Myles J. Kelleher. University Press of America, 2004.

10   Reference to Sonia Shaljean in 'Lads Need Dads: one mum's mission to save British masculinity', Martin Daubney, *Daily Telegraph*, 20 March 2018.

11   'Taken: A study of child abduction in the UK', Geoff Newiss with Mary-Ann Trayno, Parents and Abducted Children Together (PACT), 2013.

12   'NSPCC Statistics Briefing: Child Sexual Abuse', NSPCC, April 2019.

13   'Waning school discipline remains the elephant in the classroom', Peter Tait, *Daily Telegraph*, 20 March 2017, with reference to 2017 government consultation period on its guidance for expelling and exclusions in schools.

14   *Tom Brown's School Days*, Thomas Hughes, OUP, 2008.

15   'Competition in schools: good or bad?', Sue Laidlaw, Senior Partner at Laidlaw Education, *The Resident* magazine, 13 May 2015.

16   'Help your child to become a good learner', Lyn Kendall, Mensa, 11 October 2017.

17   Anti-Patriarchy Club for Boys announced in the Good Lad Initiative monthly newsletter, 24 May 2020.

18   'Guilt makes fools of the exam-passing classes – inverted snobbery and the narrative of "privilege" have made poor white British boys today's educational left-behinds', Trevor Phillips, *Standpoint*, 4 December 2019.

19   'Don't Mind Your Language . . .', Stephen Fry, http://www.stephenfry.com/, 4 November 2008.

20   'Literacy and life expectancy', National Literary Trust, 15 February 2018.

21   'The dark reasons so many rich people are miserable human beings', Catey Hill, MarketWatch, 22 February 2018.

22   'Sugar – The Facts', NHS, 11 August 2017.

23   'Number of people with obesity almost doubles in 20 years', Diabetes UK, 14 November 2019.

Adolescence

1   'Recognising adolescence', World Health Organisation.

2   *Peter Pan, or The Boy Who Wouldn't Grow Up*, J. M. Barrie, Collins Classics, 2015.

3   *The Vanishing American Adult: Our Coming-of-Age Crisis and How to Rebuild a Culture of Self-Reliance*, Ben Sasse, St Martin's Press, 2017.

4   'Labour plans to lower voting age to 16', Rowena Mason, *Guardian*, 23 January 2014.

5   'American Psychological Association Guidelines – Psychological Practice with Boys and Men report', American Psychological Association, 2018.

6   'A tyranny of its own?', Dr Stephen Blumenthal, *The Psychologist*, The British Psychological Society, March 2019. Response to the 'American Psychological Association Guidelines – Psychological Practice with Boys and Men'.

7   Reference to Randolph Nesse in 'Men die young – even if old', Betsy Mason, *New Scientist*, 25 July 2002.

8   'Number of apps available in leading app stores as of first quarter 2020', Christina Gough, *Statista*, 13 May 2020.

9   'UK gaming market worth record £5.7bn', BBC News website, 2 April 2019.

10   Reference to NPD Group in 'Kids pick mobile devices over PCs, consoles for gaming', Lance Whitney, *CNET*, 23 September 2015.

11   'More children using social media report mental ill-health symptoms', Office for National Statistics, 20 October 2015.

12 'How do we know how many children are in gangs?', Ben Butcher and Rachel Schraer, BBC Reality Check, 28 February 2019.

13 'Family breakdown makes children join gangs', Graeme Paton, *Daily Telegraph*, 17 April 2008.

14 *Beauty*, Sir Roger Scruton, Oxford University Press, 2009.

15 Sir Roger Scruton discussing why beauty matters on the New Culture Forum, 29 June 2019.

Relationships and Parenthood

1 'Average age for heterosexual marriage hits 35 for women and 38 for men', Owen Bowcott, *Guardian*, 12 April 2020.

2 'A Guide to Fertility', British Fertility Society.

3 'The Male Menopause', NHS website.

4 *Sliding Doors*, written and directed by Peter Howitt, Paramount Pictures, 1998.

5 'Facial attractiveness: evolutionary based research', Anthony C. Little, Benedict C. Jones and Lisa M. DeBruine, *Phil. Trans. R. Soc. B*, 366, 1638–59, 2011.

6 *Debrett's Guide for the Modern Gentleman*, Debrett's Ltd, 2008.

7 'Problematic Use of Internet Pornography', speaker Dr Heather Wood, Consultant Adult Psychotherapist and Clinical Psychologist at the Portman Clinic, Tavistock and Portman NHSFT, British Psychoanalytic Council, 14 July 2016.

8 'Brain activity in sex addiction mirrors that of drug addiction', Nick Olejniczak, https://www.cam.ac.uk/research/news/brain-activity-in-sex-addiction-mirrors-that-of-drug-addiction, 11 July 2014.

9 *Compulsive use of virtual sex and internet pornography. Addiction or perversion?*, In: Lectures on violence, perversion and delinquency, Heather Wood (2007). The Portman Papers Series.

10 'Lesson from History', Camille Paglia, Battle of Ideas, 14 December 2016.

11 *Brief Encounter*, directed by David Lean, Eagle-Lion, 1945.

12 'Couples who delay having sex get benefits later, study suggests', *ScienceDaily*, 29 December 2010.

13 'Does Cohabitation Lead to More Divorces?', Aaron Ben-Zeév. *Psychology Today*, March 2013.

14 'Families and Households in the UK: 2018', Office for National Statistics, 7 August 2019.

15 'Cohabitation Experience and Cohabitation's Association with Marital Dissolution', Michael J. Rosenfeld and Katharina Roesler, *Journal of Marriage and Family*, 24 September 2018.

16 *Fifty Shades of Grey*, E. L. James, Doubleday, 2013.

17 'We defend a freedom to annoy, essential to sexual freedom', *Le Monde*, 9 January 2018.

18 *The 5 Love Languages*, Gary Chapman, Moody, 2015.

19 'The Power of Vulnerability', Brené Brown, TED Talk, June 2010.

20 *The Seven Principles for Making Marriage Work*, John Gottman, Orion Spring, 2018.

21 'Announcement: The Research', The Gottman Institute, 11 February 2013.

22 'Never Give All the Heart', W. B. Yeats, from *In the Seven Woods*, 1903.

23 *Lectures to Young Men: On Various Important Subjects*, Henry Ward Beecher, Forgotten Books, 2017.

24 *The Archetypes and the Collective Unconscious*, C. G. Jung, Routledge, 1991.

25 'Cost of a child', Child Poverty Action Group, 2018.

Work and Providing

1 Finding happiness at work. Questions to ask about your job, Dan Buettner, *Psychology Today*, 21 February 2011.

2 'Homeless man found dying near MPs' entrance to parliament', Adam Forrest, *Independent*, 19 December 2018.

3 'An analysis of 2017 rough sleeping counts and estimates', Rough Sleeping Statistics, Homeless Link, 2017.

4 *Face to Face*, Tony Hancock interviewed by John Freeman, BBC, 1960.

5 'Suicides in the UK: 2017 registrations', Office for National Statistics, 4 September 2018.

Middle Age

1   *Major Works*, John Clare, Oxford University Press, 2008.

2   The Marion Gluck Clinic, the home of bioidentical hormones, established 2007. The clinic pioneered the use of bioidentical hormones to restore and maintain optimal health and hormone balance.

3   *War and Peace*, Leo Tolstoy, Vintage Classics, 2009.

4   'National Life Tables', Office for National Statistics, 2020.

5   *Down and Out in Paris and London* and *The Road to Wigan Pier*, George Orwell, Penguin Modern Classics, 2001.

6   *The Art of Happiness*, Epicurus (author), John K. Strodach (introduction, translator), Penguin Classics, 2013.

7   George Bernard Shaw quoted in *Oxford Essential Quotations*, edited Susan Ratcliffe, Oxford Reference, 2017.

8   'Living with arthritis', NHS Overview, 2018.

9   'Arthritis', Centres for Disease Control and Prevention website.

10 'Middle-aged and angry as hell? What happened when I attended a midlife anger therapy workshop', James Innes-Smith, *Daily Telegraph*, 12 September 2019.

11 'Major causes of death and how they have changed', Public Health England, 2017.

Old Age

1   'What is my state pension age?', The Pensions Advisory Service, 2020.

2   *Man's Search for Meaning: The Classic Tribute to Hope from the Holocaust*, Viktor E. Frankl, Rider, 2004.

3   Office for National Statistics: All data related to causes of death.

4   'Deaths registered in England and Wales', Office for National Statistics, 2020.

5   'Cancer mortality statistics', Cancer Research UK.

6   ibid.

7   'United against dementia: brain training and dementia', Alzheimer's Society, 2020.

8   'Connections in older age', Campaign to End Loneliness, June 2020.

9   'All the Lonely People', Age UK, 2018.

10   'No One Should Have No One', Age UK, 2016.

11   'General Lifestyle Survey 2008', Office for National Statistics, 2010.

12   'Evidence Review: Loneliness in Later Life', Age UK, 2014.

13   'Connections in older age', Campaign to End Loneliness, June 2020.

14   'Isolation: The emerging crisis for older men', Independent Age, 2014.

15   *Essays and Aphorisms*, Arthur Schopenhauer and R. J. Hollingdale, Penguin Classics, 1976.

16   'Recollections of Anaïs Nin: By Her Contemporaries', Benjamin Franklin, Ohio University Press, 1997.

Death and Legacy

1   *The Complete Poems*, Walt Whitman, Wordsworth Editions Poetry, 1995.

2   'Inspiration and Chai: Regrets of the Dying', blog by Bronnie Ware.

3   *The Art of Happiness: A Handbook for Living*, the Dalai Lama and Howard C. Cutler, Hodder, 1999.

4   *Scouting For Boys: A Handbook for Instruction in Good Citizenship*, Robert Baden-Powell, Oxford World's Classics Hardback Collection, 2001.

5   *Complete Poems*, Emily Dickinson, Faber & Faber, 2016.

If not cited above, words from Dr Stephen Blumenthal are from personal conversations with the author.

Index